FAST FORWARD

FAST FORWARD

The history of the Sydney Futures Exchange

Edna Carew

ALLEN & UNWIN

First published in 1993
Allen & Unwin Pty Ltd
9 Atchison Street, St Leonards, NSW 2065 Australia

National Library of Australia
Cataloguing-in-Publication entry

Carew, Edna, 1949– .
Fast forward: the history of the Sydney Futures Exchange.

ISBN 1 86373 5127.

1. Sydney Futures Exchange Limited—History. 2. Futures market—New South Wales—Sydney—History. I. Title.

332.645

Set in 10.5/12 Palatino by DOCUPRO, Sydney
Printed by Brown Prior Anderson Pty Ltd, Burwood, Victoria

10 9 8 7 6 5 4 3 2 1

Contents

Illustrations

Acknowledgments

Taking a book from concept to publication involves many people. Thanks are due to those who conceived the idea of compiling a history of the Sydney Futures Exchange, and whose enthusiasm for the project led to its becoming a reality. I am grateful to Ray Arthur and a chance conversation with him which led to my early involvement, to the late Desmond Brook whose initial support was a significant contribution and to Les Hosking for ensuring that the project got off the ground.

Special thanks are due to all the staff at the SFE who generously cooperated, particularly Tony Dreise, Ranald Stewart and Stephanie Maynard.

My thanks also to those who shared their memories: Clive Hall, Desmond Brook, Dick Newman, Gordon Green, Pat Nicholas, David Rutledge, John Oliver, Les Hosking, Andy McConnel, Stephen Calder, Bruce Hudson, Phil Gardiner, Clive Carroll, Bob Wright, Les Pegg, David Clarke, Ralph Watzlaff, John Currie, David Marina, Ian McGaw, Nigel Mainwaring, Ralph Carstairs, Colin Wright, Gerry van Wyngen, Warwick Poulden, Phil Gray, Chris Talbot, David Williams and to the many others who helped with historical, technical and anecdotal information.

As ever, John Hoffmann's editing skills were much appreciated.

Edna Carew
Sydney, March 1993

Prologue

Futures markets have existed for centuries. Forward trading by written contract took place in the sixth century BC in Greece; at European trade fairs in the Middle Ages, business transactions were based on a form of forward delivery document. Futures contracts, of a type similar to those used today, developed in seventeenth-century Japan.

Futures markets based on commodities emerged in the US midway through last century. Chicago, in the midst of the grain and farming belt, evolved as a natural trading centre, with its futures exchanges providing a forum where traders could take out some form of protection against fluctuations in prices of the commodities they grew, bought or sold.

The shift to financial futures is a fairly recent phenomenon which began in the US in the early 1970s and has spread increasingly around the world since then. The Sydney Futures Exchange, founded in 1960 as the Sydney Greasy Wool Futures Exchange, was the first outside the US to trade in financial futures. In its relatively short history, the SFE has evolved from a small exchange concentrating on wool futures to a global force in financial futures and options, second only to the giant Japanese exchanges in the Asia-Pacific region.

Trading in futures contracts, be they based on pork bellies or interest rates, involves assessing the future price of the relevant item and buying or selling a certain quantity of it for delivery at a specified future time. Futures traders use their knowledge of the market for their commodity when estimating its future price. Futures markets provide a regulated forum where producers, traders, hedgers and speculators trade in standardised futures contracts to protect themselves against, or make money from, fluctuations in price.

1
The legacy of an unreasonable man

The call which sealed the first trade on the Sydney Greasy Wool Futures Exchange on 11 May 1960 was the culmination of almost ten years of effort on the part of Clive Hall to see the introduction of commodity futures trading in Australia. The move provided Australian wooltraders with hedging facilities in their own country—which produced the commodity—instead of the London Wool Terminal Market which had dominated since 1953. Hall, a Sydney-based wooltrader since leaving school in 1932 (except for the war years), mounted what was virtually a one-man campaign during the 1950s to convince the Australian authorities of the importance and usefulness of such a market. He, and those who worked with him, were laying foundations of an exchange that would raise Sydney to the pinnacle of world wool futures markets and which would, by the 1980s, trade volumes of financial futures contracts ranking it among the top ten in the world.

Clive Hall recalls that the books he read as a woolbuyer in the early 1950s recommended that the appropriate place for a futures market was 'at the source of the supply'. Why, then, did Australian wooltraders deal with a distant market in London, when the world's largest source of merino wool was in their own backyard? The London Wool Terminal Market

(LWTM), opened in April 1953 and trading merino tops (a form of semi-processed wool), had followed the establishment of earlier wool futures markets in wool tops in Antwerp (1887), Roubaix-Tourcoing (near Lille, in France, 1888), the New York Cotton Exchange, which began trading in merino wool tops in 1931 and in merino greasy wool ten years later, and a market in yarn which had started in Nagoya in 1951.

These exchanges were based in northern hemisphere centres, yet most of the world's wool was produced in the southern hemisphere—Australia, New Zealand, South Africa and South America were the dominant wool exporters. Australian growers and merchants could use only the London market because of exchange-control regulations. And speculation was not permitted: they could use the London market only for genuine hedging.

The degree of seasonal fluctuations in the wool price made hedging through futures a logical method of protecting income. Hall had witnessed the wild fluctuations in the wool price in 1951. In March of that year the bottom fell out of the wool market; six months later, in October, the price doubled in two weeks—only to crash back to its earlier level two weeks later. The average price for wool in the 1950–51 selling season was 264.91 pence a pound or £360 a bale. By the following season the price had halved. Prices continued to fluctuate during the 1950s, month-by-month and year-by-year. Such unpredictable movements presented difficulties for almost everyone in the industry—farmers, wool merchants and processors. In 1952 Hall, then 39, left his job as a woolbuyer with John Vicars & Co and, with a strong conviction about the direction the industry would take, set up his own business, Clive Hall Pty Ltd, wool waste and futures brokers. At the same time, he wrote to the US exchanges for information about their futures markets. And he learned of the imminent establishment of a wool futures exchange in London. The decision to start a wool futures market there was based on the volume of trading; the London wool sales were regular and many wool merchants and processors bought their supplies there. But there was no processing of wool in London. Early in the 1950s, the prominent wooltrading house J.W. McGregor & Co—which had good international links—arranged for Hall to travel to the US and to London to see the newly established London Wool Terminal Market in operation. During Hall's time in the UK, his zeal led the Bradford *Wool Record* to dub him Australia's 'Mr Futures' (as did *The Bulletin* later in Australia). The UK paper said that 'in the tradition of his countrymen he stood up to the fast-bowling very stolidly and, in return, knocked a few British objections for six'. On his return, Hall set about extolling the advantages of hedging. A number of major Australian exporters, processors and even some big growers were persuaded to use the London market.

To help spread the word about the new futures markets and to emphasise that their primary purpose was price protection, the US firm Nichols & Co Inc sent to Australia an ambassador for wool futures, Bob Cossaboom. J.W. McGregor—which represented Nichols in Australia—sponsored a series of seminars in June 1953 in the Australian capital cities. Clive Hall, having studied wool futures in the Boston, New York and London offices of Nichols & Co, shared the podium with Cossaboom at the seminar in Sydney's Australia Hotel.

The opening of the LWTM gave Australians their first chance to protect themselves against wool price movements. However, Hall, using the London market as an associate member, found that there were drawbacks to trading in a market on the other side of the world and in a different time-zone. Also, London traded wool tops, which were several stages away from raw wool, and the prices of the two did not necessarily move together. Mindful of the advice he had read—that a futures market should be at the source of supply—Hall began what was to be a single-minded, and virtually single-handed, campaign during the rest of the 1950s to get an Australian wool futures market off the ground. He believed that the rightful place for Australian wool futures trading was in Australia, dealing in an Australian product in Australian currency and in Australian time. And, aside from his own background and experience, he knew that a futures market in wool was a more attractive proposition than one in, say, wheat, because wool was the only commodity free of government pricing and marketing controls.

To be successful, an Australian wool futures exchange would need international support because the wool market relied on international, as well as domestic, trade. During the 1950s, Hall made several trips to the countries which were major consumers of Australian wool, such as the US, the UK and Japan, and discussed his ambition with everyone who would listen. Those who doubted that a Sydney futures market could succeed based their views on a conviction it would be sellers-only. As E.R. (Bob) Howells, later general manager of the exchange's first clearing house, wrote in *An Outline of Futures Trading* (1961): 'The inference [was] that if producers (or sellers in any form) shared the general view that the price of wool would rise they would refrain from the use of futures. If, on the other hand, it was generally thought that prices would fall they (the sellers) would be unable to find matching buyers.' Howells wrote that the argument was weak because

> supply and demand if given free expression will always bring buyers and sellers together at a common point . . . World trade recognises no national boundaries and if in the exigencies of the moment two futures markets dealing in the same or closely related commodities (such as wool and wool tops) move out of line arbitrage operations will bring them back into relative balance.

Hall talked to H.C. (Nugget) Coombs, then the head of the Commonwealth Bank (at that time, and until the Reserve Bank began operating in 1960, Australia's central bank). He conferred with trade officials and politicians in Canberra and emphasised to government leaders the potential importance of a wool futures market in Australia. He made frequent trips to the national capital for interviews with the then Treasurer, Harold Holt, and others. For more than five years, Hall poured time, money and energy into a tireless endeavour to stimulate interest in wool futures. He even succeeded in capturing the Prime Minister's attention. Hall was one of 30 guests at a dinner for Sir Robert Gordon Menzies at the Union Club in Sydney late in 1958. After dinner the guests were permitted, two at a time, to join Menzies in the smoking room for two minutes. Hall got his word in: 'Sir, what about a wool futures market in Sydney?' Menzies replied: 'You mean similar to the cotton exchange in New York?' 'Yes,' said Hall. 'Send me something in writing,' said Menzies. Enthused, Hall was writing at dawn the next day, setting out for the Prime Minister the virtues of futures markets.

His cause was helped, he says, by the fact that Australian interest in wool futures had increased in 1958–59 following sharp price fluctuations at wool auctions. There were growing arguments for some mechanism to minimise the effects of these changes. The federal cabinet established a government inquiry into the viability of a wool futures market. But Hall was impatient for progress. On 2 August 1959 he wrote to a former schoolmate, Bill (later Sir William) Gunn, who had just been re-elected chairman of the Australian Wool Bureau:

> It appears that there is strong opposition from the London end. No doubt the boys there are afraid that they will lose business to an Australian market and will do all they can to exert influence one way or another to block it . . . I was in Melbourne last Thursday and saw a number of senior people in the trade and to all of them and to others in Sydney I put the same question, which was, 'Did they know of any valid reason or objection to the establishment of an Australian greasy wool futures market?' None of them had anything concrete by way of reply other than that they had read somewhere there would not be enough support for the market. I feel myself that people are getting confused on this issue; surely if private enterprise in the form of a number of firms are willing to put up their money and start a greasy wool futures market, it is their affair whether it works or not.
>
> I was delighted to hear that you were re-elected Chairman of the Australian Wool Bureau and I wondered if you had any further news for me on the Wool Bureau's attitude to futures and to a local futures market using their valuations on wool in Australia.
>
> Time seems to be passing rapidly and we are still not getting anywhere on this market.

Hall's letter provoked some action, and on 16 September he wrote again to Gunn:

> I was delighted to see in *Queensland Country Life* that you have been outspoken in favour of futures. I think a lot will depend on the decision of the Australian Woolgrowers' Council next week as to which way the Government moves.
>
> It might interest you to know that recently a member of the Committee of the London Wool Terminal Market Association has written to me advising me that his Committee have promised their whole hearted support to an Australian

> market. I have also had advice from America, indicating that they would not only use it for arbitrage purposes but also for direct business, similarly verbal indications strongly in favour from Japan.
>
> I also have nine initial floor members standing by, ready to act in the event of a Government decision being favourable. Rules and regulations of both the Clearing House and the Futures Exchange have also been drafted and in the event of a favourable Government decision we would immediately invite a member of both the New York and London Markets to come out in an advisory capacity.

Hall was succeeding in making waves. The 17 September 1959 Hansard records the Minister for Air, David Fairbairn, querying during question time when a decision might be made:

> I ask the Prime Minister whether he has seen the statement made this week by the chairman of the Australian Wool Bureau, Mr Gunn, advocating the establishment in Australia of a wool futures market. Is he aware that a number of other graziers' leaders also have advocated the greater use of wool futures as a means of reducing the violent fluctuations which occur in the price of wool? Is it a fact that an application was made to the Government some months ago for permission to start a greasy wool futures market in Sydney, with nine original floor members? When is it expected that a decision will be made on this application?

Hall was appreciative of having the issue raised in parliament but conscious that very few people, apart from Gunn, had openly said they favoured a wool futures market. He continued lobbying for public support. On 29 September he wrote to Gunn:

> The thing that is concerning me at the moment is that there has been no announcement from the Woolgrowers' Council about their decision not to oppose a futures market in Australia. If this could be made public it would assist materially the case for futures at present, particularly when set out beside the AWC's strong opposition to a floor price.
>
> Could you tell me if there is any particular reason for them not making this decision public? I feel sure Frank Skelsey of *Queensland Country Life* would be interested to hear it, as would the other country papers.
>
> It would appear that the Government is leaving no stone unturned in their investigation about futures at the moment and I feel there is a body somewhere working strongly to get

> that business put to London, which I think you will agree is just plain stupid. We have the opportunity right now to establish a greasy wool futures market in Australia which would very quickly become a big market and ultimately the biggest of its kind in the world.

Hall finally received a letter from Holt, dated 18 November 1959, granting approval for the Sydney Greasy Wool Futures Exchange to go ahead. The wooltraders had been sceptical about the likelihood of government approval, and news of the Treasurer's letter took them by surprise. Its tone was fairly neutral: 'The government does not express any view, and in fact was not called upon to do so, as to the advisability or otherwise of your proposal in respect of a greasy wool futures market . . . exchange control approval would be provided to enable floor members to engage in appropriate arbitrage operations in wool futures markets overseas.' Hall had got the green light he had been seeking for almost a decade.

Within a week of receiving Holt's letter, he called a meeting of representatives from the nine firms he had approached and who had said: 'If you get exchange-control approval, we'll be in it.' The nine Hall had selected, and his own firm, were the founding floor members of the infant futures exchange. Hall had wanted to include a Japanese firm as a founding member, given Japan's role as a major buyer of Australian wool. But memories of the war in the Pacific were still influential then, and the others rejected the suggestion. The ten firms represented at the inaugural meeting to form the futures exchange, held on 25 November 1959, were:

Anselme Dewavrin Fils et Cie
W.P. Martin Whittingham Pty Ltd
Wilcox Mofflin Ltd
Lempriere (Aust) Pty Ltd
K.V. Chapman & Co Pty Ltd
Kreglinger & Fernau (Aust) Pty Ltd
Wm. Haughton & Co Ltd
J.W. McGregor & Co
Dreyfus & Co Ltd
Clive Hall Pty Ltd

These ten became the founding members of the Sydney Greasy Wool Futures Exchange; Hall had chosen them because they would provide worldwide coverage for the new exchange. However, it was clear that more would be needed to provide a market of adequate size and depth and the founding members agreed to offer an additional five seats. So rapidly had enthusiasm for the concept grown that Hall received 28 applications. At a meeting on 8 January 1960, a committee, including Clive Hall as founding chairman of the proposed exchange, chose an additional five floor members (again, no Japanese firm was included):

Nichols (Futures) Pty Ltd
Simonius Vischer & Co
R.G. Bailey & Co (Aust) Pty Ltd
Herbaux and Masurel (Aust) Pty Ltd
G.H. Michell & Sons Ltd

The early Sydney Greasy Wool Futures Exchange (SGWFE) followed the London model and invited members of the wool trade to become associate members of the exchange and trade wool contracts at half the commission rates that applied to non-members. Hall recalls that it was 'most encouraging to us to receive applications for associate membership from trade houses in a number of wool-consuming countries such as the UK, Japan, Belgium, France, Italy and the US'. The exchange also received applications for associate membership from local woolbuyers and sellers and some trading banks. It admitted 114 associates, each of whom paid £500 for membership.

The first meeting to decide how the exchange would operate was held in the offices of the merchant bank Development Finance Corporation at 16 O'Connell Street, Sydney. Several measures had to be in place before the new market could open. Members would have to provide financial support, arrange a clearing house and secure central bank approval to remit funds to non-resident accounts. The authority given to the SGWFE regarding the movement of funds was unique at that time; prevailing exchange controls did not permit an easy inflow or outflow of funds. Exchange-control approval was essential to the operation of the new market because 90 per cent of Australian wool was exported, and non-resident participation was vital because of the lack of local knowledge about commodity futures trading. The exchange-control approval also covered arbitrage deals provided that, in inter-market transactions, one leg of the deal was based in Sydney.

Hall approached the London Produce Clearing House (forerunner of the International Commodities Clearing House) to clear the Sydney wool futures contract (the chief function of a clearing house is to guarantee the performance of obligations entered into on an exchange). The London-based company responded that it would not be appropriate to offer clearing facilities, pointing out that it would have been difficult to provide senior management in Sydney and that the clearing house functioned most efficiently and economically when it could handle several markets in one place for the same, or broadly the same, clearing membership. Sydney was offering only one market. There was speculation in Sydney that the UK company was reluctant to be associated with a contract that would compete with the London market or that it simply had little faith in the Australian market's chances of survival. An acceptable clearing house was found locally when a subsidiary of Development Finance Corporation, Australian Development Clearing House Pty Ltd (ADCH), agreed to clear for the new exchange. ADCH, which was separately capitalised and independent from the SGWFE, continued to clear for the SGWFE until 1969.

Considerable effort went into drafting the early articles and by-laws, which were modelled on the London exchange and, to a lesser extent, on New York. The next important step for the SGWFE was to make itself known to other major futures markets around the world. In December 1959 Clive Hall and Bob Howells, a senior representative of the clearing house, undertook a round-the-world trip to promote the exchange. Hall later said they were generally well received and encouraged in their venture 'with perhaps the exception of the London market members whose fears appear to have been justified'.

While overseas, Hall got word of a proposal by the Australian government which could endanger his yet-to-be-born exchange. The government was planning to tax the profits accruing to non-resident futures traders. Such a move would have deterred the overseas interest vital to the market's growth. Once back in Australia, Hall confronted Holt and explained that, since futures traders took orders from others on behalf of clients whose identity was not revealed, it would be impossible to know whom to tax. The tax proposal was dropped, as Holt confirmed to Hall later in a letter.

The SGWFE was incorporated under the NSW Companies Act on 25 January 1960. A copy of the certificate of incorporation was tabled at a management committee meeting on 11 February. The exchange was established as a non-profit organisation with the liabilities of its members limited to a nominal sum should it be wound up. Conditions of membership were residence in Australia, a deposit of £5000 and an annual subscription of £100, with the deposit to be returned should membership be terminated. There were two classes of members, floor and associate, and day-to-day administration was in the hands of the management committee. The committee advised that the new exchange had secured office space in Delfin House at 16 O'Connell Street—conveniently, the premises also housed the clearer, ADCH.

Finding a celebrity to open the SGWFE took some time. At a meeting on 18 February, Clive Hall said he had written to the Prime Minister, requesting him to officiate at the formal opening on 11 May. But Menzies was due to travel overseas. The acting PM, Harold Holt, felt the demands of the job would keep him in Canberra. The Lord Mayor of Sydney was also to be out of the country. The honours fell to Robert (later Sir Robert) J. Webster, chairman of Felt & Textiles of Australia Pty Ltd, then the biggest wool processors in Australia. Webster, having some understanding of futures markets, was a suitable candidate. On 9 May, two days before the opening, a cocktail reception was held in the Rainbow Room of the Australia Hotel. Invitations were sent to some 300 guests, to be entertained at an estimated cost of 30 shillings a head, including drinks. The invitation list included 150 members of the NSW and Queensland Wool Buyers' Association, two members of each of the wool-selling brokers' associations, two representatives of the trading banks, one representative from each associate member, one member of the auditors and one from the solicitors, the chairman and secretary of the Stock Exchange of Sydney, one representative from each of the local mills, a representative from each of the local woolscourers and fellmongers, the chairman of Development Finance Corporation or his representative, one representative from the clearing house, three representatives from each floor member,

The Sydney Greasy Wool Futures Exchange's first trading floor, on the 5th floor at 16 O'Connell Street, in the heart of Sydney's business district.

including one or more floor operators, and the press. A further 25 invitations were for the chairman's own initiative.

The first office of the SGWFE, with a full-time staff of four, was on the fifth floor of 16 O'Connell Street. Nearly half of the exchange's meagre space was occupied by its 30-foot-square open-outcry trading floor, furnished with tiny booths that allowed no privacy (doors and windowed partitions came later). A visitors' gallery, with room for five or six people, was no more than a section of the trading floor separated from the activity by a rope. Trading in wool futures began on 11 May 1960. The contract was for the greasy wool equivalent of 3000lb of clean wool, a size that put the market comfortably within reach of the small grower while still being attractive for arbitrage on the London and New York markets.

The exchange opened at a time when there were no experienced floor traders in Australia. Some members brought staff with the necessary experience from the UK and they were able to help in training local traders. Among the newcomers from London in 1960 were Desmond Brook, Gordon Green and Michael Breen, all of whom had joined the wool futures market in the UK in 1953 when the LWTM opened, and Doug Bates, a senior official at the LWTM whom Hall and Howells had hired in London to be the SGWFE's first secretary. Brook was first drawn to the commodities industry in the early 1950s when, while on military service in Singapore and Malaya, he met a number of people associated with the UK commodities house Lewis and Peat, which was involved in tin and rubber. Back in London, he joined a Bradford-based company, Richard Fawcett & Sons, handling the firm's business in London and dealing with clients in the UK, Europe and the US. His task in Australia was to establish and manage the Australian operations of the Belgian-French wool futures broking house Herbaux and Masurel, one of the founding floor members of the SGWFE. In 1963, Herbaux and Masurel merged with another founding member of the SGWFE, R.G. Bailey and Co (Aust) Pty Ltd, forming BHM (later BHM Futures Pty Ltd), which Brook continued to run.

Gordon Green came to Australia with R.G. Bailey. He recalled answering an advertisement the company had placed in 1953 for a teleprinter operator. 'Disabled serviceman may suit', the advertisement had said. Green, who had been pensioned out of the navy, applied for the job. Michael Breen was hired by Wilcox Mofflin Ltd and after four years joined W.P. Martin Whittingham Pty Ltd. Breen developed a formidable reputation as a chartist; his specialisation in straddles later prompted Jim Sinclair, managing director of International Commodities Clearing House, to christen him 'the straddles king'.

Trading on the first day of business for the SGWFE amounted to 140 contracts. The first month's business totalled 980 contracts but by the end of 1960 it was not unusual to see 3000 contracts traded in a month. About 60 per cent of the business came from outside Australia, with support from the UK and the US, Europe, Japan, South Africa and New Zealand. The French tended to be mostly sellers, while Bradford merchants were big buyers of wool futures. US interest waned with the rise of synthetics. And initially trading with Nagoya was difficult because, while Japanese regulations allowed funds into the country, they did not permit funds to be taken out, so profits had to stay in Japan— and no interest was paid. However, the Japanese were big buyers of Australian wool and, in recognition of this, a Japanese company, Kanematsu-Goshu, was admitted as a floor member of the SGWFE in 1961.

Participants included merchants, traders, wool-buying houses and mills hedging stocks or forward sales, and professional commodity traders and woolgrowers, who represented less than 5 per cent of open contracts. Some woolgrowers and members of the wool trade did not like the idea of futures because they believed futures trading depressed auction prices and could be subject to manipulation.

The merchants accounted for most of the business. Farmers were never big users of futures and their lack of interest was a disappointment to futures markets. Active participation in futures markets by farmers was not encouraged by the banks or the wool-selling brokers. Grower attitude to futures was summed up by the Bureau of Agricultural Economics in its 1963 *Wool Economic Research Report*:

> Growers' objections to futures trading, other than the categorical refusal to be associated with 'speculation' are mainly based on the fear that futures may depress wool prices, or may reinforce price fluctuations, or that the market may be manipulated at the expense of unwary users. Yet it appears that there is neither theoretical justification nor positive statistical evidence for price effects disadvantageous to growers.

The same paper had some compliments for the SGWFE.

> During nearly three years of operating, the Sydney Wool Futures Market has attracted sufficient interest at a growing rate to make it safe to predict that it has come to stay. Economic success generally points to some need, conscious or latent, that had been waiting to be filled. In the case of the wool futures market that need is varied and complex because different people with their specific functions engage in futures transactions for different purposes and often for a multiplicity of purposes.

Desmond Brook later noted in a paper *The Role of Wool Futures in Price Determination* (March 1991), that the Australian Wool Corporation also considered using the market:

> As an important trader of wool, the Corporation would benefit from the right to operate on the Sydney Futures Exchange. Its operations would be far too extensive for the SGWFE to be

Founding chairman Clive Hall (centre) discusses the script of a documentary film about the SGWFE with Doug Bates, the exchange's secretary (left) and Stuart Glover of Visatone Television Pty Ltd, director of the film which was scripted by John Pearce, the exchange's public relations officer.

> able to provide adequate hedging facilities to cover all of its forward trading activities and the stocks of wool sold, but occasions could arise on which commercially oriented futures trading activities would be warranted. In addition, it would also be appropriate for the Corporation to be able to use its futures operations as a price stabilising influence.

Four of the five members admitted by the first selection committee in 1960 were overseas-based and had a substantial worldwide customer base, reflecting the international flavour of wool trading. During the years when wool was the dominant interest of the Sydney exchange, Desmond Brook spent a minimum of two months each year overseas, drumming up business. With some 60 per cent of trading-floor business originating overseas, it was important to keep in touch with foreign clients. He recalled that his client base was in Japan, Europe, UK, US, South Africa and New Zealand:

> It was an enormous international trade. Australia could be

Clive Hall (right) presents Gordon Green (left) and John Pearce with diplomas certifying they were qualified commodity traders, having completed a correspondence course on futures sponsored by the Association of Commodity Exchange Firms of New York (forerunner of the Futures Industry Association).

> supplying the wool to Bradford; Bradford could turn it into the wool tops and export it to France; France turned it into yarn and exported it to Italy; Italy could make it into cloth; the cloth was exported to the US; the US make it into a suit and export it to Japan. That's the sort of thing that could happen, and with risks all the way along, prompting hedging and other commercially based trading.

The fledgling exchange took promotion of its business seriously. In 1960 it hired its first public relations officer, John Pearce (who after about a year with the SGWFE resumed his career in radio). While with the SGWFE, Pearce scripted and narrated a documentary film about the exchange's activities which was used to demonstrate to Australian woolgrowers how futures markets operate. Equipped with an expensive projector, Pearce travelled throughout Australia, lecturing about futures markets to often hostile audiences. Woolgrowers generally viewed this showman from the SGWFE as representative of city-slickers out to rip off the farmer. Pearce's film was also used as promotion to overseas purchasers of Australian wool, and copies were sent to the US and Japan. Pearce and Gordon Green were the first in Australia to undertake a correspondence course on futures sponsored by the Association of Commodity Exchange Firms of New York (the forerunner of the Futures Industry Association, the leading group representing the futures industry in the US). Clive Hall visited John Pepion, president of the association, who agreed that material relating to delivery on US exchanges could be deleted from the course, bringing its cost down from $US100 to $US60. On completing the course, Pearce and Green received diplomas certifying they were qualified commodity traders.

As the chairman reported in March 1963, expenditure on promotion was heavy, a development that he regarded as unavoidable in what he called 'a critical [year] in the development of the exchange'. The chairman commented:

> During the year turnover fell on the exchange by over 4000 contracts compared with 1961 but this was during a period when all world commodity markets were having a lean time, as well as stock exchanges . . . However it was quite noticeable that despite our low turnover in the latter part of the year, our daily figure started to show greater turnover numerically than on other world wool markets, Nagoya excepted.

As part of its campaign to spread the word, the SGWFE had its *Australian Futures Reference Book* translated into Japanese, a lengthy task undertaken by Jim Morita of C. Itoh. Hall and Howells travelled to Japan to launch the book.

The advantages of using the SGWFE were becoming recognised. The October 1962 *Quarterly Review of Agricultural Economics* included an article discussing the cost and benefit of hedging wool:

> According to the method of measurement adopted in this study, short hedging on the Sydney market during the two years of its existence would seem to have reduced the price risk by about 40 per cent with better protection on large losses than on small ones. Though protection afforded by short

Portrait of founding chairman Clive Hall by renowned Australian artist Clifton Pugh, presented to Hall by exchange members to mark his first term as chairman.

hedging was better in London, the performance of the Sydney market has tended to improve both relatively and absolutely.

To mark his first term as chairman, Hall was presented by the exchange members at a dinner at the Hotel Australia with a portrait of himself by the renowned artist Clifton Pugh. The painting now hangs in his Sydney home.

Activity continued to develop during the ensuing years, with Sydney becoming established as world leader in setting the wool price. The market grew steadily, but did not really come of age until 1963, when up to 12 000 contracts were being traded in a month, and Sydney had developed a name as a force in wool futures markets. Between 1964 and 1972 the exchange enjoyed a period of growth and consolidation that made it the world's leading wool futures market. However, by the second half of the 1960s a grave threat to the wool futures contract was emerging, with speculation that a reserve price for wool was on the horizon.

In 1965, though, futures business was booming at such a rate that the SGWFE was bursting out of its premises; it moved to another floor in the same building, acquiring 2500

The second home of the Sydney Greasy Wool Futures Exchange, on the 3rd floor at 16 O'Connell Street. The exchange remained there until 1969, when it moved to Australia Square.

square feet. The new trading floor was opened by the Minister for Housing, Leslie Bury, on 14 April 1965. The opening was celebrated by Clive Hall, the exchange's vice-chairman Ken Chapman, and a number of guests including Bob Howells from ADCH, Alistair Urquhart, chairman of the Sydney Stock Exchange, Pat Nicholas from the Australian Woolgrowers Council and John (later Sir John) Marks, chairman of Development Finance Corporation. The exchange remained at 16 O'Connell Street until 1969, when it moved to Australia's state-of-the-art office tower, the new Australia Square, where it occupied 4000 square feet on the seventh floor.

By 1966, the SGWFE was conscious of a need to evaluate future directions. Hall's inquiries about who would be the best person to provide advice led him to contact a US academic and authority on futures markets, Professor Roger Gray of the Food Research Institute at Stanford University. Hall arranged for Gray to visit Australia to undertake a review of the SGWFE and lecture on the mechanics of futures trading. In a foreword to Gray's report, *Wool Futures Trading in Australia—*

Further Prospects, Keith (later Sir Keith) Campbell, wrote: 'It appeared that the Sydney futures market had reached a stage in its development where a critical evaluation by a recognised world authority on futures trading would be valuable.' While Gray was in Australia, Hall mentioned his latest idea: a futures market trading a share-price index. 'You're one hundred years ahead of your time, Hall,' was Gray's reply. Hall had not received an encouraging response from the government about this proposal. Prime Minister Menzies had written in November 1965 that, regarding the proposal for a share-price index exchange, 'it would not appear on this occasion . . . that there are any aspects on which the Commonwealth could comment'. Menzies continued:

> This, no doubt, arises from the fact that trading in company shares in the Australian States whether on a futures basis or under existing arrangements, is conducted under State law and the rules of the stock exchanges and is outside the Commonwealth's constitutional powers. You will also appreciate, I feel sure, that it would not be appropriate for the Commonwealth to express any general view on the proposal.

The SGWFE changed its clearing arrangements in 1969 when its contract with ADCH expired. Ian McGaw, manager of the London Produce Clearing House, had accepted an invitation the previous year from Desmond Brook, then running Bailey Herbaux Masurel, to come to Sydney and see the SGWFE's operations. Consequently, LPCH suggested that it was now equipped to handle the Sydney clearing business, having overcome earlier misgivings and significantly upgraded its computer services. LPCH established a branch office in Sydney, so that the SGWFE's contractual relationship was with the London company, providing a far stronger clearing-house guarantee than could have been available from an Australian subsidiary.

By the end of the 1960s a reserve price scheme had become a matter not of 'if' but of 'when'. Wool price support schemes had progressively decreased the need to hedge on the futures exchange against price fluctuations. Then, in 1972, after a period of collapsing wool prices, came a turning point: the formation of the Australian Wool Corporation and the establishment of a reserve price scheme for wool under which the corporation supported a floor price (reviewed each year) by

Clive Hall (left) encouraged prominent visitors to the exchange to learn about futures markets. Here he hosts a visit in 1982 from Bill Hayden, federal leader of the opposition.

buying wool in the market. With wool producers assured of a minimum price, there was little need to hedge. Activity on the exchange went into decline—ironically at a time when wool was once again booming. By 1972, six out of the original fifteen members had quit: Lempriere, Wm Haughton & Co, Wilcox Mofflin, Martin Whittingham, J.W. McGregor and Dreyfus & Co. Some were replaced and the new roll-call of members read: Bailey Herbaux Masurel (BHM), Booth Newman, Chapman, Clive Hall Pty Ltd, Dewavrin, C. Itoh, Kanematsu, Kreglinger, G.H. Michell, Nichols and Simonius Vischer.

It was clear, though, that the exchange would have to expand its product range to survive. Preparations began in the early 1970s for the introduction of a cattle contract and work began on the long haul towards establishing a currency futures market. Wool continued to increase steadily in volume until 1973; during the boom conditions of that year the exchange was trading about 1700 contracts a day. Then, except for a brief period in 1980, turnover declined and, by 1990, trading in wool futures, the original backbone and *raison d'être* of the exchange, was virtually dormant. The wool contract remained physically deliverable until 1986, when it became cash-settled, a change driven partly by the costs associated with delivery, including testing charges, core sampling and weighing, hand sampling, selling brokers' handling charges and appraisal charges. The suspension of the reserve price scheme for wool in 1991 raised the possibility of a revival in trading wool futures.

At the end of the exchange's first two decades, the industry acknowledged the man whose efforts during the 1950s had resulted in the establishment of a futures exchange in Australia. The tribute in the 1981 annual report to Clive Hall included some lines from Rudyard Kipling:

If you can fill the unforgiving minute
With sixty seconds' worth of distance run
Yours is the Earth and everything that's in it.

The tribute ended: 'And Kipling's words

If you can wait and not be tired by waiting
If you can dream and not make dreams your master

aptly describe the patience, persistence and dedication with which the Sydney Futures Exchange, as we know it today, was founded and developed into the vibrant, living entity it now is.'

In January 1982 Clive Hall retired, ending more than twenty years' association with the exchange. At a black-tie dinner held in his honour, Phil Gardiner, then chairman of the SFE, gave a speech and hailed Hall as one of the world's much needed 'unreasonable men'. Drawing on a quote from the playwright George Bernard Shaw, Gardiner said:

The reasonable man adapts himself to the world; the unreasonable one persists in trying to adapt the world to himself. Therefore all progress depends on the unreasonable man.

2
Currency futures—out of the money

During 1971 shifts were occurring in worldwide financial arrangements that were to have a significant impact on the Sydney Greasy Wool Futures Exchange. The year was a watershed for foreign-exchange markets, signalling the end of what was known as the 'Bretton Woods' era of fixed exchange rates and the progressive introduction of floating exchange rates. Floating exchange-rate regimes had existed previously, in the late nineteenth century and during the 1930s, and were enjoying new support by the early 1970s, particularly among academic economists and free-market proponents such as the US's Milton Friedman. They believed that floating exchange rates would bring stability in currency markets and argued that markets were better able than governments to determine appropriate exchange-rate levels.

The Bretton Woods system, introduced after the Second World War, was in some ways similar to the earlier gold standard, which had operated from about 1880 and had established fixed exchange rates, with the levels of various currencies set in relation to gold. Under the Bretton Woods system exchange rates could move, but only within narrow bands and only in specific circumstances. Most currencies in the Bretton Woods system were tied to the $US, which remained convertible into gold. However, by the late 1960s confidence in the $US was waning; the US had issued more paper money than could be backed by gold and when, on 15 August 1971, the US government announced it would no longer redeem paper for gold, the Bretton Woods system was clearly finished. In December of that year central banks and treasury officials put together a replacement; under this 'Smithsonian Agreement' the official price of gold rose from $US35 to $US38 an ounce, effectively a 7.9 per cent devaluation of the $US. And the American dollar was no longer convertible into gold. However, the lack of confidence in the $US continued and strong-currency countries, such as Switzerland and Germany, were flooded with unwanted dollars as investors exchanged the weak $US for francs and marks. The Swiss, with a strong currency backed by gold, withdrew the Swiss franc from any parity with the $US. A further devaluation of the $US had minimal effect. In March 1973, when the foreign-exchange markets started dumping the $US and sterling, the major trading nations agreed to close the markets to review the situation. When the markets re-opened several weeks later, any pretence of holding exchange rates within official limits had been abandoned. The fixed exchange-rate system had collapsed and rates between the $US and other currencies were free to float in line with supply and demand.

The volatility of interest rates in 1971, rising inflation and confusion in foreign-exchange markets had not gone unnoticed by the US futures markets. It was becoming clear that the kind of risk that challenged a commodities producer or trader also confronted banks, borrowers and lenders. Thus in 1972 was born the first futures exchange that would trade solely financial futures contracts—the International Monetary Market (IMM), an offshoot of the Chicago Mercantile Exchange. The IMM was the brainchild of Leo Melamed—the powerful chief of the CME and the man who became known as the 'father of financial futures'. Melamed engaged support from leading academics such as Friedman for the development of financial futures. The currency and interest-rate contracts were structured by Mark Powers, then product development officer at the CME. The IMM began trading in seven foreign-currency futures contracts.

Australia in those years operated with a fixed exchange rate and a network of exchange controls that strictly regulated the inflow and outflow of funds. Until December 1971, for historical reasons, the $A was pegged to sterling. Between December 1971 and September 1974 the $A operated on a fixed link with the $US. Under this 'fixed peg' system the $A maintained a constant relationship with the $US but varied in its relationship with other currencies. By the end of the year the $A had been revalued against the $US to a level of $A1 = $US1.2750. Controls on capital inflow to Australia were tightened and a variable deposit requirement (VDR) introduced on overseas borrowing.

Those at the helm of the SGWFE had been monitoring the overseas developments and, in 1972, conceived the notion of introducing a currency futures contract on the Sydney exchange as a way to help importers and exporters better manage their cashflows. In preparation for this they had already registered a new company, Sydney Commodity Futures Exchange Ltd, incorporated on 21 September 1971. The Sydney Commodity Futures Exchange Limited was to form another company, Sydney Currency Exchange Limited, to manage the currency futures operations, but all activity associated with the market would come under the umbrella of the Sydney Commodity Futures Exchange Ltd. At that stage, a notional starting date was 1 June 1972, which would give ample time to complete legal formalities and invite applications for floor membership.

Campbell Robson, secretary of the SGWFE, and Jim Sinclair, managing director of the clearing house, met Reserve Bank of Australia (RBA) officials in February 1972 to outline the exchange's thoughts about a currency futures market. The negotiations were to be protracted. The RBA made it clear that there was no chance of establishing a futures market in foreign currencies along the lines of that operating in the US. Transactions in foreign exchange were limited to the trading banks and the RBA imposed restrictions on the purposes for which Australian residents could buy foreign exchange. The suggestion that the proposed futures market could operate in $A equivalents of specific amounts of foreign currencies would not contravene RBA policies but it was pronounced potentially unworkable for an entirely different reason: such a market would not involve delivery of the commodity and thus could contravene prevailing gambling laws. In the light of the RBA's exchange-control policies, discussions centred on a 'notional foreign currency futures market'. The RBA would not commit itself but conceded it 'might be possible for the exchange to operate a notional foreign currency market without requiring any authorities under the Banking (Foreign Exchange) Regulations'. The exchange went ahead with plans to establish a currency futures market trading the equivalent of overseas currencies ($US, yen, sterling and Swiss franc) in Australian currency, and presented its submission to the RBA on 28 April 1972. In an accompanying letter, the exchange said that 'the approval now sought is an extension of that notified by the Treasurer in his letter of 18 November 1959 to Mr C.M. Hall'. This extension would provide automatic approval for remittances to and from overseas. In support of its proposal, the exchange argued:

> The formation of this market will bring added maturity to the Australian capital market scene . . . We believe it is in Australia's interests to take the initiative in this field and develop a centre of operations for the initial benefit of commerce in this region. For this reason the Sydney Greasy Wool Futures Exchange Limited intends to broaden the base of operations of its internationally respected wool futures market, by the introduction of an internationally oriented currency futures market. As with the wool contract, the currency contract will play an important role in international dealings, assisting Australian status in world finance affairs at a time when the Australian government is negotiating for status in the major decision-making bodies of the Group of Ten and OECD [which Australia had joined only in 1971] . . .

The exchange began advising members of the exploratory work undertaken to establish a currency futures market, indicating that the RBA had suggested 'there might be no insurmountable problems in the way of a market in notional foreign currency futures' although the central bank emphasised that it could not be definite in its attitude until it saw the exact form of contracts and delivery procedures.

The exchange followed its submission with a letter in July to the RBA governor, John (later Sir John) Phillips. The governor replied promptly, hoping that he would 'soon be able to advise their attitude'. The exchange made no public announcement about its intentions but did send a circular to associate members, including the 53 overseas members. Changes were in the wind regarding foreign investment, which the SGWFE believed enhanced prospects for its proposal.

On 2 August, Jack Wright, then adviser to the RBA governor, told the exchange that the proposal had been through all the channels at the RBA and been forwarded to Treasury. He unofficially advised the exchange's secretary, Campbell Robson, that the RBA was in favour of the proposal with the exception of local participants acting on an arbitrage basis on US markets, and with the exception of any implied suggestion that the RBA would supply the exchange with the mandatory close-out rate of exchange. On the same day, Desmond Brook, then deputy chairman of the SGWFE, wrote to the secretary of the Treasury, Sir Frederick Wheeler, offering assistance if that would speed up finalising the project. The letter was followed by a telephone call on 15 August to an assistant secretary who promised 'attempted finality by 23 August'. On that date, another telephone discussion elicited the information that the matter was now in another Treasury division but it would try to finish by the end of the month. First assistant secretary Brian Fleming, returning from sick leave, promised to try to keep that deadline. Later in the month, the SGWFE learned that its proposal was now with the International Relations Department of Treasury. A telephone conversation with Fleming on 1 September revealed that no conclusion had been reached and there was every likelihood of further delay. Foreign exchange and capital flows were generating much interest in parliament at that time, and not wholly in ways favourable for the SGWFE's proposals. That month, controls on the outflow of capital were slightly relaxed, with Australian residents allowed limited portfolio investment overseas. But controls were reintroduced on the inflow of foreign funds, prohibiting overseas borrowings for terms of less than two years.

At a meeting early in September between Campbell Robson and RBA officials, Robson canvassed the possibility of the exchange's hurrying the process by opening a currency futures market confined to transactions between Australian residents. He was told that while there seemed to be no legal impediment to this it could prove difficult to keep out non-residents and any broker handling non-resident business would need the appropriate approval from the RBA. The exchange noted in its record of the meeting: 'RBA officials were embarrassed at the approval delay [from Canberra] . . . So far as RBA concerned the exchange is proceeding. RBA confirmed delay possibly because of new political implications.' During the meeting Robson sought confirmation of his impression that the RBA was basically favourably disposed to the exchange's submission. In its customary neutral language the RBA told him there was 'no reason for him to think the RBA's attitude had changed'.

In anticipation of the move going ahead, the floor members voted at an extraordinary general meeting on 22 September to alter the name of the exchange from the Sydney Greasy Wool Futures Exchange Limited to the Sydney Futures Exchange Limited. (Later, in 1982, the SFE reserved the name Australian Futures Exchange in case that should become more appropriate.) The articles of association were also amended to provide for additional markets. The exchange was hopeful of introducing the new contract by the end of 1972 and was considering inviting Sir Robert Askin, Premier of New South Wales, to open the market. On 29 September the SFE's solicitors wrote to the Chief Secretary's Department of the NSW government, outlining the exchange's intentions to establish a currency futures market:

> As you will immediately appreciate the setting up of a futures market dealing in foreign currencies anticipates conflict with the Commonwealth Banking (Foreign Exchange) Regulations but we do appear to have found a method acceptable to the Reserve Bank of so operating the proposed market that such regulations are not breached. By inserting provisions in the contracts to be traded on the proposed market which have the effect of eliminating the actual delivery of the foreign currency in specie the Banking Regulations are not infringed.
>
> However, this very step has highlighted a difference of opinion between solicitors and senior counsel which seems capable of solution only by legislation, and it is for that reason that we are writing to you to seek the views of the state government of NSW.
>
> The problem, stated briefly, is whether the contracts traded on a futures market constitute a Contract of Wagering or Gaming capable of being struck down under Section 16 of the Gaming and Betting Act, 1912 . . . What is proposed, therefore, is an amendment to Section 16 of the act so that excluded

from the operation of the section will be contracts traded on such futures markets as may be approved . . .

On 17 October, Brian Fleming told the exchange that the project had been completed in Treasury and was on daily notice to the Treasurer. No lengthy delay was anticipated. The exchange noted that neither Treasury nor the RBA had indicated a negative attitude to the proposal in the course of these discussions. According to Desmond Brook, their plan was quite well received. 'No one said we were talking rubbish, or told us to go away,' he later said.

Encouraged, the exchange began to plan the launch of its new contract. The working committee charged with getting the currency futures market into action pursued a hectic schedule. The proposed currency contract was drafted in October, in cooperation with the exchange's solicitors, and changes to the by-laws were discussed. The committee met representatives of the major banks, traders, merchant banks and other companies, outlining the proposed contract and canvassing interest. It recommended a contract of $50 000 Australian equivalent of the overseas currency, probably trading $US, sterling, yen and Swiss francs, with the market non-deliverable. Advertisements calling for floor and associate members would be placed in January. A report covering membership requirements and details of the proposed contract for the Sydney currency futures market was circulated during December.

A press conference held at the exchange's premises in Australia Square on 12 December 1972 opened with an announcement by SFE chairman Dick Newman that the Sydney Futures Exchange was to launch the first international currency futures market outside the US. Also attending were deputy chairman Desmond Brook, secretary Campbell Robson and the manager of the clearing house, Jim Sinclair. Newman delivered a lengthy explanation titled *What is futures trading?* and took questions from the floor. In answer to 'Do you have to satisfy the Reserve Bank people?', Newman replied: 'We have naturally been in touch with the Reserve Bank and they have not discouraged us.' Another question: 'Do the Reserve Bank think what you are proposing is a good idea?' Newman answered: 'The Reserve Bank was very non-committal as ever, but they could have squashed the idea very rapidly if they wanted to. They don't necessarily at this stage disapprove of it.' The following day's newspapers carried reports of the proposed new market in Sydney, 'the first international currency futures market outside the US'.

By January 1973 the SFE was receiving applications for membership, with considerable interest shown by banks, merchant banks, import and export businesses and foreign banks. The 7.05 per cent devaluation of the $A against the $US in December, combined with greater flexibility in exchange-rate movements in major economies, had apparently increased the interest of potential users in the new contract. Those expressing interest in trading the new market as floor members were the AML&F group, Hill Samuel Australia Ltd (later Macquarie Bank), Foreign Exchange Brokers (Patrick Partners), Jackson Graham Moore & Partners, Gollin Holdings Ltd , MBC International (later BA Australia), Carruthers & Co, First Chicago Australia Limited, Australian Investment & Development Ltd, and Throgmorton Securities Ltd. Those applying for currency associate membership included the merchant bank Partnership Pacific Ltd, G.H. Michell & Sons (Australia) Pty Ltd, A.J. McConnel, the Commercial Banking Company of Sydney, Ord BT Co Ltd and Darling and Company Ltd. Despite growing concern about the continued delay in official government approval for the market, the exchange had decided to close applications on 30 March. In a circular to the SFE board, dated 12 April 1973, Campbell Robson advised that, to determine the order in which the ten applicants for floor membership would be put forward at an extraordinary general meeting on 16 April, each director was to complete an order of preference for admission to membership. The preferential sequence was necessary because of the board's recommendation that, while all ten applicants were suitable, only eight new floor memberships would be created. With new members lined up, the exchange was euphoric about the imminent realisation of the goal which had taken so much effort.

At 5.15pm on Friday 13 April the SFE's plans were knocked completely off the rails. The exchange was verbally informed by Lin Wilson, manager of the Reserve Bank's exchange control department, that the government had slammed the door on the proposal for a currency futures market. The decision was conveyed to the RBA governor by telex from Sir Frederick Wheeler, secretary of the Treasury. A letter from Wilson, written that day and received at the SFE on the morning of Monday 16 April, confirmed the stunning rejection:

> It has now been decided that exchange control approvals in relation to participation by non-residents in the proposed currency futures market will not be forthcoming. We have also been asked to inform the Exchange that the Government will not look with favour on the establishment of a currency futures market even for trading confined to Australian residents.

Nervous that any further action on a currency futures market could jeopardise existing arrangements for the wool futures contract, the SFE decided that the agenda for the extraordinary general meeting scheduled for 9.30 that morning should be allowed to lapse. According to the minutes, Andy McConnel, an associate member of the exchange and a director representing associate members, reported that he had:

> . . . conducted some inquiries over the weekend through sources of his and the decision had been made by Treasurer Mr Crean, and opposition had arisen to the proposal only when it had processed itself to the Policy Department of Treasury. Apparently the major feature which led to the rejection was the fear that the Currency Market would provide a medium for speculation in the Australian Dollar, whereas our case was that the Market would prevent speculation in the Australian dollar . . .

The futures exchange faced a dilemma. On the one hand it had received encouraging response from applicants for membership who wanted specifically to trade the proposed currency contract; on the other, it had no wish to go against the express wishes of Treasury and the government. The SFE could have gone ahead, without the need for official approval, with a currency futures market for domestic use only. What did require approval was non-resident participation and the movement in and out of Australia of funds—and overseas participation was regarded as crucial to the market's success.

Some, including Desmond Brook, believed the exchange should have proceeded with the contract. 'There was nothing really to stop us, and the contract would have boomed once started,' he later said. 'And we would have prevented the development of the hedge market. But in the event we did not proceed, although the legalities had been cleared [regarding settlement of the contract].' In Brook's view, the contract would have appealed to small importers and exporters. 'It was a big setback for the exchange,' he said. He ranked the retreat from starting a currency futures contract at that time as one of the major mistakes made by the exchange. Others agreed with him, then and later, particularly the new members who had been willing to support the contract.

On Monday 16 April, following the tabling of Wilson's letter, Dick Newman, as SFE chairman, had the dispiriting task of writing to all prospective members, informing them 'with regret' of the turn of events. Newman said that Jack Wright later confided that the RBA had expected the SFE to defy the government and set up the new market. And Wright pointed out that approval for the movement of funds was an RBA, not government, matter, and that the RBA was not about to withdraw the existing approvals for the wool contract.

At a meeting of floor members and recommended applicants for membership on 1 May, Newman said he believed the concept of a currency futures contract had commercial approval at both Reserve Bank and Treasury levels, but it fell short on policy grounds pertaining to the Australian dollar. 'It would be difficult to change the decision, and we therefore must provide an excuse for the decision to be changed,' Newman told the meeting. The SFE could not jeopardise the position of the wool futures market, although it was keen to examine all avenues for furthering the establishment of currency futures. It had been suggested to him that the currency futures project had 'become involved in part of an internal politics power struggle within the Public Service and hence the somewhat hot and cold treatment of the concept'. The RBA had confirmed that the currency futures proposal had run into problems in Canberra after being cleared by the Reserve Bank. A representative of Foreign Exchange Brokers suggested a deputation to the RBA and Treasury to determine exactly why the proposal had been rejected; a representative of Throgmorton Securities emphasised that work must be continued on the project 'to keep the pot boiling'. The exchange was clearly not about to roll over and accept the rejection of its proposal.

Newman pointed out that the exchange, in the course of working on the proposal, had had difficulty finding people who had a grounding in both foreign exchange and futures. Clive Hall commented that the circumstances recently experienced were parallel to those of the original application made in 1959. 'At that time Cabinet rejected the original application through a lack of knowledge of the concept of futures,' Hall said. 'As a result, the Department of Primary Industry made an inquiry and on referral back to Cabinet the exchange controls were approved. The same circumstances exist today.' Several of those attending were pessimistic about a government change of heart, one commenting that his understanding was that the Treasurer, Frank Crean, had no wish to see Sydney develop as a major financial centre of the Pacific Basin.

The SFE had widespread support in the business and financial community. In a letter dated 23 May to Campbell Robson, the representative in Australia for The First National Bank of Chicago, Harrison Tempest, had some advice:

> My own view is that had each of the proposed members of the exchange been Australian-owned companies, the exchange would have had a much better chance of approval with the present Federal Treasurer. Of course, we all recognise that for the market to be viable here, overseas interests must be imminently involved. However, my strategy if I were in your shoes would be to gather together the most 'Australian' of those interested in the exchange and go to Mr Crean and ask him under what conditions he would approve the establishment of the market. I think you will find that, despite your best efforts, nobody down in Canberra really understands what the exchange is about . . . However, if you approach [Crean] on the basis that the market is designed to make the Australian dollar a more acceptable international currency in line with his wishes, and that instead of operating to speculate against the Australian dollar the market would support the Australian dollar you may meet with more success . . . in summary I would say the approach should be Australian companies will be in control of the exchange and will only involve overseas interests as a 'necessary evil' in making the market operate.

At a meeting between SFE officials and staff from the RBA's exchange control department on 6 June, Dick Newman suggested that a lack of knowledge at Treasury of futures markets had been a contributing factor to the decision made on 13 April. Lin Wilson of the RBA agreed, but added that, in his view, that was only a minor factor in the overall decision. Following further discussions with the RBA, it was decided that a new submission should be sent direct to the Prime Minister, Gough Whitlam, and Treasurer Frank Crean; it should not discuss market technicalities but should address the advantages the proposed market would bring Australia. And the SFE should engage a professional consultant to compile the submission, such as Philip Shrapnel Pty Ltd.

Dick Newman wrote to Prime Minister Whitlam on 23 August with the submission prepared by Philip Shrapnel & Co, *The need for a currency futures market in Australia,* and included a request for an opportunity to elaborate on the principles involved. On the same day Newman also wrote to the governor of the Reserve Bank, enclosing a copy of the submission and informing him that copies had been sent to the Prime Minister, the Federal Treasurer and the NSW government.

The governor responded on 5 September: 'We appreciate being kept informed and are particularly grateful for the copy of the document prepared by Philip Shrapnel & Co Pty Ltd.' Newman had to wait until 29 November for a response from the Prime Minister, who apologised that it was 'not yet possible to send you a substantive reply on the matter'. Whitlam continued:

> The proposal advanced is of some complexity and falls within the ministerial responsibility of my colleague the treasurer. I therefore feel it would be more appropriate for the treasurer to respond to the proposal on behalf of the government. I have told Mr Crean that I am ready to consult with him on the matter should he consider this to be necessary.

Crean responded on 7 February 1974. His brief letter concluded:

> Although your renewed proposals deal with a number of points of detail which, earlier, had not been fully clarified, they appear to introduce no new material of substance which would lead me to a judgment different from that which has already been conveyed to you.
>
> I must therefore inform you that the advice already provided to you on this matter stands. The necessary exchange

> control approvals will not be given and the government will not look with favour on the establishment of the market you propose.

The letter was signed by Crean, a Labor traditionalist with no time for financial markets and opposed to speculation in the currency; the sentiments were also identified as those of John Stone, then deputy secretary (economic) and later secretary of Treasury. Stone, who did not favour any move to free up the exchange rate, was particularly opposed to a currency futures market as being inconsistent with prevailing arrangements for setting the exchange rate. Newman replied on 6 March, conveying the 'disappointment of the board'. He added: 'The proposed market has created genuine interest in a broad range of commercial and financial companies, and the view has been firmly expressed that such a market is a necessary adjunct to present day business requirements. Because of this it is the intention of the exchange to seek a review of this decision at a later date.' In view of the finality in tone of Crean's letter, which arrived almost ten months after the original refusal, Newman on the next day wrote to those who had expressed interest in membership of the currency futures market. He attached a copy of Crean's letter, refunded the fees that had been placed with the exchange as part of the application process and thanked all those involved for their enthusiasm and support.

However, Newman did not give up. His lengthy correspondence with Treasurer Crean was not yet over. In July, Newman wrote again, saying that while the SFE board had accepted the government's decision, it was anxious that the concept not be permanently shelved. 'An influential cross-section of the Australian business community still considers the formation of this market desirably essential to its needs, and has commended the exchange in its energy and enterprise over the last two years, in its efforts to achieve the market's formation,' Newman wrote. His efforts won a a six-line response from Crean within a week, saying the Treasurer had noted Newman's request that, should circumstances change, discussions could be opened up again.

In Newman's view, such a change occurred some weeks later, in September, when the Australian government decided to devalue the $A by 12 per cent, cut the fixed link with the

$US and have the Australian exchange rate determined by a trade-weighted basket of currencies so as to maintain a constant overall value against the currencies of its major trading partners. He wrote that the exchange 'would appreciate a re-examination of our proposals and your favourable reply to our request for exchange control approvals'. Crean replied on 14 October:

> I fear . . . the underlying assumption on which your letter is based is not in accordance with the facts. The government's decision . . . to determine the exchange rate for the $A in future by reference to changes in an average of foreign currency value weighted in accordance with trading significance to Australia, does not carry any implication of 'possibly moving towards a more freely determined basis'. On the contrary, the government's decision . . . means that our exchange rate will actually be more 'fixed' than it was previously, when it was in a sense 'floating' (in line with the float of the $US) . . . it is a change towards greater stability in the rate rather than greater fluctuation. Against this background, I therefore see no grounds for a re-examination of the proposals previously put by the Sydney Futures Exchange Ltd.

And so ended two years of effort.

Events in foreign-exchange markets were far from standing still in the years that followed, nor had the SFE given up on its proposed currency futures contract. As Desmond Brook said in a paper, *Towards a currency futures market*, delivered in October 1977 at a conference in Melbourne:

> Inhibited by policy attitudes, the SFE sat on the sidelines and observed, to its frustration, increasing costly proof of the need for the facilities its proposal offered. Devaluation and more frequent currency changes, the development and growth of the 'grey' market, the increasing difficulty in obtaining forward exchange cover, its cost to the public and the way in which the SFE's more recent proposal stimulated similar proposals endorses the belief that the SFE's original concept . . . [had] undeniable appeal . . .

Brook was referring to the growth of the currency hedge market. The regimented form of forward cover available through the banks' 'official' forward market had inspired some enterprising minds to devise a more flexible alternative—the currency hedge market. This market catered for those ineligible for the banks' market, which was constrained by a number of rules. For example, anyone with a forward exchange risk had to seek cover within seven days of incurring the risk, the Reserve Bank was unwilling to provide forward cover beyond six months and the banks' market was available only to Australian residents seeking cover for trade transactions. Capital transactions were not eligible. The hedge or 'grey' market developed in the early 1970s when several Australian companies began informally arranging cover of currency exposures among themselves. Settlement was in $A.

The SFE's efforts to establish an alternative to the forward cover offered by the banks had provided a catalyst for the currency hedge market by bringing together like minds who identified advantages in getting such a market more widely used. Among these were Howard Michell, whose company G.H. Michell, one of Australia's largest processors and exporters of wool, was aware of the problems caused by shifts in the value of the currency. Another was Peter Phillips of what was then Meares & Phillips. In 1976 the two formed Meares Michell Pty Ltd, later acknowledged as the pioneer of the foreign-currency hedge market, which grew from an estimated $50 million in 1975 to $250 million in 1977. A leading player in the hedge market in those early years was the stockbroking firm Jackson Graham Moore. Meares Michell in 1976 was joined by Elders Finance & Investment Co Ltd; the newly formed Meares Michell Elders traded nationally and had a major role in the developing currency hedge market. MME disbanded early in 1978 when two chief operators, Phil Gardiner and Ken Stockton, left to join the merchant banks Hill Samuel Australia and Schroder Darling. The two merchant banks became forces in the hedge market; others active included Michell Finance Pty Ltd, Jackson Graham Moore and two individual operators, Ralph Carstairs in Sydney and Roger Wilson in Melbourne.

The market developed outside the banking system and operated by enabling two parties with opposite exposures in foreign exchange to agree to a mutual offset of risk. Each indemnified the other against loss if the exchange rate moved to a level other than that agreed upon. The grey market provided a popular solution to the commercial risks involved when dealing with foreign currency and filled a gap left by the inadequate forward cover provided by the banks.

Conscious of the development of the currency hedge market and aware of the ground already lost, the SFE invited those still interested in establishing a currency futures market to a meeting on 14 July 1976. Desmond Brook was in the chair. Dick Newman, having presided over earlier attempts to introduce currency futures, summarised the events since April 1974. Many of those at the meeting favoured dusting off earlier submissions, updating the Shrapnel report and making a presentation to a senior level of government. Neville Kidd, David Clarke and Malcolm Phillips, representing the AML&F group, Hill Samuel and MBC International, said their companies would be willing to contribute financially towards any investigations by the SFE. The exchange was encouraged in its renewed endeavours by changes that had occurred since the Labor government had rejected its earlier proposal. By late 1976 capital and trade transactions were being inhibited by a widespread view that the $A was overvalued, an opinion vindicated in November that year when the year-old Fraser Liberal government announced a 17.5 per cent devaluation of the currency. Such a massive, sudden move highlighted the importance of hedging. The SFE felt the time was opportune to renew pressure for a currency futures market.

Eric White Associates, in its role as consultant, offered some advice: 'Critical to success will be the support and influence of commonwealth Treasury. Clearly—for what reasons we do not know—it was in Treasury that the original proposal foundered in 1972/73. We know that the Reserve Bank is not opposed to establishment of [currency futures] . . .'

Several meetings followed in late 1976, involving Desmond Brook, Jim Sinclair as head of International Commodities Clearing House (ICCH) and Jack Wright, formerly adviser to the RBA governor and by then retired. Wright had advised Dick Newman, in a letter dated 3 August, to 'go ahead . . . If, however, you prefer to try again for government "blessing" I think you need to present a short crisp case. I do not think the Reserve Bank need any convincing but I see no change in the Treasury attitude . . .' A few weeks later, John Stone addressed a meeting of the Council for the Economic Development of Australia (CEDA) and a member of the audience took the opportunity to put a question to him about Treasury's attitude towards a currency futures market in Australia. The gist of his answer was related to Malcolm Phillips next day in a note:

> Mr Stone spent some considerable time in talking about overseas countries and their experience in this area, but he finally made the personal statement that, after his four years experience with the International Monetary Fund, he had come to the conclusion that currency futures markets were not in the best interests of the community as a whole, although they may be of benefit to individual sectors of the community. He therefore was not in favour of the setting up and operation of a currency futures market in Australia.

Stone's response was given at a time when, following the first 'oil shock' of 1974, international financial markets were being buffeted by massive flows of short-term funds. His words reflected a conservative view, dominant in the Fraser government at that time, that it was in Australia's best interests to insulate the economy as much as possible from the consequences of these developments—although the government and its advisers were mindful that their capacity to do so was steadily shrinking.

In another letter, dated 28 October, Wright wrote to Newman:

> Unfortunately, Dick, the change in government has not involved any change in the people determing exchange rate and other economic policy. Continued failure of policies persisted in must in due course force politicians to over-ride the failed advisers, but the delay causes irreparable damage to industries, the unemployed and our international markets. It is for this and other reasons that I wish you luck in your efforts to get one break in the 'Stone' wall.

The exchange was bolstered in December by news that the government had asked Treasury to examine ways to provide cover against forward exchange risks other than the limited facility already offered by the banks. The original SFE proposal had been mentioned as a possible alternative. 'It also appears that Treasury are resisting this direction, although the reasons are unknown at present,' Desmond Brook wrote in a memo on 7 January 1977. However, the SFE had the impression that there was now no opposition from either the government or the ALP to the concept of a currency futures market. In early February, without publicity, the SFE sent a new submission to Canberra.

The SFE attended a series of meetings with government departments and senior government advisers, the RBA and the Australian Bankers' Association. By May 1977 it was an open secret that the exchange had sent its proposal to senior government figures, including Treasurer Phillip Lynch and Prime Minister Fraser. It was widely recognised that the SFE's chief obstacle was Treasury, which viewed the exchange rate as an important instrument in economic policy and which remained reluctant to relax its control even to a limited extent. Progress again seemed stymied. Expressing the frustration felt by many, Malcolm Phillips, a long-term supporter of the currency futures contract, wrote to Dick Newman that he was 'of the opinion that we are almost to the stage where we have to make a decision as to whether we should go ahead and set this market up regardless of Treasury.' Phillips continued:

> It seems to me we are really asking for the impossible if we expect Treasury to go out of their way to assist us in creating such a market. I believe the Reserve Bank and others have done everything they can to see that nothing prevents us from moving ahead. Whilst I believe your exchange has given Treasury some undertaking, this does not apply to others. Could you, therefore, let me know whether you think it would be possible for the market to be established by someone other than the Sydney Futures Exchange, in such a way that the original plans for running it were not altered.

Silence continued from Canberra. In August, an exasperated Clive Hall wrote to Prime Minister Fraser, asking for a brief meeting to discuss currency futures. Fraser expressed interest and referred Hall to the Treasurer. The SFE had decided to concentrate its efforts on influential members of government, rather than bureaucrats. Hall and Sinclair were cordially received by Phillip Lynch on 2 November 1977 but, with cabinet preoccupied by a looming election, it was made clear that the SFE would have to wait. The exchange had been waiting ten months since first putting its proposal to the Treasurer and rival interests had been gaining ground, with talk rife that the banks were gearing up to provide additional forward cover facilities. The SFE's case won something of a boost early in 1978 when Everett B. Harris, then president of the Chicago Mercantile Exchange, took up Clive Hall's invitation to visit Sydney and, in the words of one supporter of currency futures, 'assisted in throwing light on futures and currency futures in particular'. Also, the SFE had decided to widen its support net and invited additional merchant banks to join the informal currency committee. By this stage, the SFE could cite reasons for both optimism and pessimism. John Howard, who had taken over as Treasurer from Phillip Lynch in November 1977, was by all accounts favourably disposed to the SFE's proposal. Moreover, the proposal had been in government hands for a year, and not yet been rejected. The government was known to be examining two proposals for foreign-exchange cover, one from the SFE and one from the trading banks. The banks' submission was their first; for the SFE, it was the third. Some interested parties believed that the government was about to come to a decision; others, conscious that Treasury was still unwilling to cede any of its influence on the $A, believed the issue could remain in limbo for months.

On 12 January 1979 Clive Hall, once again chairman of the SFE, received a letter from Howard saying that 'this government would not act to hinder any business proposals that are within the law . . . any organisation which commenced trading in currency futures at the present time would have to do so on the basis of existing exchange control policy. As you know, this excludes non-resident trading and arbitrage transactions by residents in overseas markets for this purpose'. The news prompted Jack Wright to send a letter to the editor of *The Australian Financial Review*:

> Sir, Your striking front-page and thought-provoking editorial (15 January) first shocked me with just what the Treasurer had, in fact, agreed to for the currency futures market.
>
> I was just about to let my elation at the brief reports in other papers fool me into sending around congratulations at what seemed like a surprisingly sensible, albeit belated, 'market' concession by this disappointing 'free enterprise' government.
>
> As an adviser to the governor, Reserve Bank, with responsibility in this field, I chaired an international committee (including a senior Treasury representative) which saw merit

> in a proposal for such a market when it first reached a developed stage about 1972 (4 governments ago). I did not think it needed any Reserve Bank or Federal Government approval. It did not involve actual exchange dealings and required, perhaps, only State clearance under 'Gaming and Betting', surely a mere formality.
>
> Yet it got to Canberra to get a 'liberal' government's blessing . . . and got itself held up by the Treasury, largely on the prejudices for keeping power in Canberra of one senior Treasury official. Fairly obviously that same official, who is now nearing the 'top', despite what I see as a succession of policy 'victories' that have been disastrous, both for Australia and the ministers he has dominated, has had written into Howard's announced decision at least two deadly conditions.
>
> What your paper disclosed was that the new 'market' must exclude arbitrage with international markets and keep out all 'non-residents'. These were two restrictions which we had earlier said would make a real market impossible. How could other exchanges, commodity markets etc function without any participation from abroad? Perhaps we should not have given the bureaucrats and other opponents (eg, banks holding on grimly to their exchange dealing monopoly) this clear hint of how to give a phoney 'go ahead' . . . I wish the currency futures market success, and an early death to its shackles, to repay the long, patient, courageous and skilled efforts of its sponsors.

Dick Newman, no longer chairman of the SFE but still a board member, and managing director of Booth Newman Pty Ltd, wrote to Wright on 31 January thanking him for his help and encouragement. Newman commented:

> I fear we were too naive in 1972; we probably asked too much and then lost the initiative and were not able to come back to the government to modify our request. I was very interested in your background comments, but I fear the stonewalling would have been too strong for us to overcome.

The SFE could now move to resolve any problems with the NSW state government regarding the Gaming and Betting Act. In February 1979, NSW Treasury established a working party to examine the issues and options associated with the proposed currency futures market. Its report canvassed three issues:

- the level of encouragement the government might wish to

Clive Hall, exchange chairman in 1980, explains currency futures trading to British Consul-General A. H. Spire, CBE, on the first day of trading in sterling futures on the SFE, 26 November 1980.

give to a market that could further enhance Sydney's role as a financial centre;

- the question of removing doubts occasioned by the Gaming and Betting Act; and
- the question of government regulation of futures markets.

The working party identified several alternatives, which included 'do nothing', amend section 16 of the Gaming and Betting Act, take a legislative approach to regulate and control futures markets or exclude futures markets from the provisions of the Gaming and Betting Act, with approval of the currency and commodity markets being dependent on ministerial approval of their rules and regulations. The latter was favoured as it brought a degree of regulation without involving continued and detailed supervision. The Futures Act of NSW was passed in November 1979, exempting currency futures from the Gaming and Betting Act and thus enabling the currency futures contract to trade.

After years of frustrated attempts, the SFE began trading currency futures in March 1980 when it launched $US and yen futures contracts. John Howard, last in a long line of treasurers whom the SFE had urged to permit currency futures, had given his assent and agreed to open the new contract on the SFE trading floor. Launching the new contract, Howard paid tribute to 'the enormous patience of people like Clive Hall, and others who waited upon the government over a period of some years'.

The choice of $US and yen seemed logical, given Australia's trade links with Japan and the fact that much trade is $US-denominated. The high hopes that had long been held for currency futures were to go unfulfilled. The yen contract was suspended in 1981 because of a disappointingly low level of activity. Sterling futures, introduced later in 1980, were suspended early in 1982 for the same reason. The $US futures contract performed best of the three but was overhauled in the mid-1980s and subsequently traded as a $A contract.

During this time, the banks tightened their grip on the foreign-exchange markets. There was little market share for the Sydney Futures Exchange. A chapter in the history of currency futures closed in June 1984 when the Sydney Currency Futures Exchange Limited was voluntarily wound up. It was an unspoken acknowledgment by the SFE that despite its marathon run, it had missed the boat.

3
The golden years—rorts and high-rollers

Long before it embarked on its drawn-out endeavours to foster a currency futures market, the exchange had been conscious of a pressing need to diversify. Wool had enjoyed a boom until the early 1970s but the introduction of a floor price threatened the exchange's only commodity. Business could ultimately dry up. As early as 9 December 1971, the board minutes record a discussion of a 'multi-commodity exchange' that would trade wool, a beef futures contract and eventually other contracts. An investigating committee was established to look into the potential of a beef futures market. The group included chairman Dick Newman, Phillip Hentze, Desmond Brook, Campbell Robson, Jim Sinclair as secretary and David Rutledge who, having studied under Roger Gray in the US, had been coopted to advise on technical matters. The exchange made a submission to the Australian Meat Board on the 'desirability of introducing a uniform system of grading and/or classification under the present system of marketing beef in Australia'. (Ultimately, the exchange's decision to launch a cattle contract was the catalyst for a national livestock classification scheme.) The committee evaluated three types of beef contract: live cattle, frozen boneless beef in cartons and chilled carcase beef (the committee was meticulous: it debated the alternative spellings of *carcass* and *carcase*, consulted the literature on the subject and settled on *carcase* as its official style).

Little interest was shown in the boneless beef project. In May 1974 the exchange dropped the idea, conceding that the physical market was not big enough, and, after considering chilled carcase beef, proceeded with plans for a live cattle contract. Among the hurdles to be overcome was the difficulty of defining a live cattle contract in Australian conditions, which tended to result in irregular types of cattle and a natural lack of uniformity of cattle grade. The board approved the introduction of a live cattle contract on 23 December 1974, with the objective of launching the new contract in mid-1975. New associate members joining to trade the live cattle contract included Ataka (Australia) Pty Ltd, Toyomenka (Australia) Pty Ltd, Twynam Futures Pty Ltd (a company owned by cattle king John Kahlbetzer, also a major wool player), Kibby & Burchell Futures Pty Ltd, Constable & Bain, AML & F, J.W. McGregor Wool Company and Howes Holdings Pty Ltd. The then Commercial Banking Company of Sydney Ltd (later merged with the National Bank) came in later as an associate member.

Cattle prices were booming when work began on the contract but, by the time it was introduced in July 1975, prices had begun a slump that was to last until a return of buoyant conditions in 1979. The contract initially called for the cattle to be slaughtered for delivery but this proved unsuccessful so the by-laws were changed to enable delivery of live cattle. The revamped contract began trading in July 1977, and received a boost a year later when the US President, Jimmy Carter, announced a shortfall in US beef imports. Australia was allocated a large quota, which saw prices improve. By 1979 cattle was trading between 300 and 960 contracts a day.

Meanwhile the SFE had been busy amending its by-laws to accommodate a change in the wool contract from greasy to micron wool. Greasy wool was phased out over twelve months and a futures contract based on micron wool began trading in July 1977.

Discussions were also under way that led to the introduction of a gold futures contract. By the mid-1970s financial conditions worldwide had become volatile, with inflation and interest rates rising and exchange rates fluctuating. The $A underwent a large devaluation in 1974 and another in 1976. International investors were increasingly turning to gold as a safe haven in uncertain times. The market gained momentum in 1974 when the US government allowed US citizens to buy and hold gold for the first time since 1933. In 1975 the International Monetary Fund abandoned an official gold price and allowed central banks to trade gold in the open market. In the following year the Australian government relaxed restrictions on individuals holding gold. That year, the gold price began rising, boosted by a round of big OPEC oil-price rises. At the same time, inflation was eating into the domestic purchasing power of the $US and investors sought gold as a hedge. At the SFE Clive Hall, Dick Newman and Desmond Brook recognised that the introduction of a new contract such as gold would bring a new dimension to the exchange. Hall started making his own inquiries about a gold coin or bullion market and a silver bullion market. The exchange subsequently established a committee with a brief to get a gold contract going. Andy McConnel, who had first joined the SFE as an associate member in 1972 and had served on the board and who, since 1975, had been a principal of the broking firm and floor member Ross McConnel Kitchen, was appointed convenor of a gold futures formation committee. Members included Bert Aitken, a director of Matthey Garrett Australia, who provided technical advice, Geoffrey Robinson, then director of the Perth Mint, and Paul McNab, a director of Harringtons Metallurgists. McConnel and Brook undertook the groundwork for the contract, drafting regulations for Australia based on the by-laws of the New York Commodity Exchange (Comex) gold contract (which had begun trading in 1974) and opting for a contract half the size of that traded on the giant New York exchange. McConnel recalled that the word from the Reserve Bank—through the pragmatic Jack Wright—was that there would be no problems in the way of the gold contract, provided it was restricted to a domestic market and did not involve non-residents. McConnel said that the RBA was 'fairly accommodating' in its definition of a non-resident and accepted the SFE's argument that the exchange received orders from local offices but could not know every source. A potential setback arose when the Metric Conversion Board told the SFE that the gold contract could not be dealt in troy ounces but would have to be in grams. McConnel protested that troy ounces was the standard used by gold dealers worldwide and to deviate would seriously affect the viability of the market. That was accepted.

Discussing the proposed gold contract at an extraordinary general meeting of floor members on 1 February 1978, chairman Clive Hall said that action was required or 'we may wither on the vine'. New blood was needed and currency members, a matter also under discussion, would certainly provide that. With their contribution, and some self-help, the exchange could become 'a modern financial institution', Hall said. At that meeting Hall also indicated that new floor members could pay 'around $25 000' entrance fee—a sum that Hall thought was 'reasonable' and which the market could bear. Such fees from new floor members, he noted, together with possibly 100 new associate members, would raise about $500 000 for the exchange to finance the first two years of operation of a currency futures market.

Contract specifications for gold were adopted at a board meeting on 15 February 1978 and the by-laws adopted on 1 March. McConnel wrote to International Commodities Clearing House (ICCH), formally requesting it to clear and guarantee the contract. On 3 March the SFE announced the gold contract would start trading the following month and reported a lengthy list of new associate members who had joined to trade gold futures. These included Meares & Phillips, Harringtons, the Australian Bullion Company, the Commercial Banking Company of Sydney, J.W. McGregor, G.H. Michell, Bain & Company, Elder Smith Goldsborough Mort, E.F. Hutton & Co London, Merrill Lynch, Ord Minnett, Robert Crann & Green and SBC Australia.

Gold was already in demand when the SFE launched its gold futures contract on 18 April 1978; at that time, it was fetching $A156 (about $US200) an ounce. The launch of the new contract by the Lord Mayor of Sydney, Leo Port, ushered in a new era and a new image for the SFE, broadening its appeal and attracting a new kind of trader. Until the arrival of gold, the bulk of the SFE's traders were connected with, or interested in, the rural sector. Most futures trading was undertaken by a fairly close-knit network of companies which had a hands-on interest in the physical commodities traded. This situation changed dramatically after 1978. Gold caught the attention of a far wider range of players that included the general public and the futures speculator.

Interest in the new contract accelerated almost from day one. Merchant banks were quick to identify the arbitrage opportunities, with several active in profitable gold cash-and-carry transactions. In these, a merchant bank borrowed funds to buy the physical gold, sold gold forward on the futures market and, after allowing for margins and other charges, profited from the difference between the cost of the borrowed funds and the gold transaction. The general public was also quick to climb on the gold bandwagon, getting into the market through brokers such as Ross McConnel Kitchen, Jackson Graham Moore & Partners and Robert Howes & Associates which, in the late 1970s, handled the lion's share of retail futures broking in Australia. The SFE acquired a substantial gallery of punters.

A growing taste for gold was turned into an insatiable appetite in 1979 by events which were felt worldwide: political tensions, especially in the Middle East; concerns about the short-term prospects for the US economy and uncertainty about the $US; rising inflation in most developed countries (pushed up by regular OPEC oil-price increases); a distrust of paper currencies; a move by international investing institutions and wealthy individuals to include gold in their assets; and a trend among Middle Eastern nations whose oil revenues were mounting to buy and hoard gold rather than invest in the US where Iranian funds had been frozen and the domestic currency was shaky.

Gold hysteria gripped speculators. The price began to soar, feeding a worldwide boom that in turn provided enormous growth for the world's gold futures markets. A rush to buy became a tidal wave which caught up people from all walks of life. Australians were not left out. SFE volumes soared. Activity in gold attracted new floor members to the exchange. In February 1979 Harringtons Metallurgists Pty Ltd joined and was followed a month later by a crop of financial bluebloods that included Australian United Corporation Ltd, BT Australia Ltd, Elders Finance & Investment Company Ltd, Hill Samuel Australia Ltd and Trans City Holdings Ltd, all paying the exchange's new $25 000 entrance fee—a price that was to appear a bargain when compared with the price of membership in subsequent years. (For example, in 1983 Bailey Herbaux Masurel sold its seat to Barclays Australia Ltd for $355 000; in 1988 Barclays sold the seat for $1.6 million.)

By mid-1979, speculation was rife that gold could cross the magic threshold of $US300 an ounce. Excitement was mounting. The forecasts were fulfilled in August 1979 when the gold price hit a new record of $US324, its rise fuelled by speculative buying from the US, the Middle East and Asia. Trading on the Sydney Futures Exchange reflected the world mood and turnover in the gold contract climbed to 700 or 800 trades a day—levels that would be dwarfed in ensuing months. By September the SFE had hit a new record of 1209 trades in a day and the gold price was heading for $US400, incidentally dragging silver prices in its slipstream. When the SFE's volume hit another new high of 1741 contracts in one day, ICCH acknowledged the increasing risks of trading gold futures by lifting the deposit on the gold contract from $750 to $1000. Late in September the gold price came off the boil and drifted down to around $US375; activity on the SFE took a corresponding dip to under 1000 contracts a day.

The lull was shortlived. The frenzy resumed and on 1 October the metal topped $US400 in New York and Hong Kong. The next day saw more hectic trading: the gold price rose by $US30 and hit $US437 in London, an increase of $US120 over the previous month. In Sydney, 3056 contracts were traded on the SFE, worth about $50 million—almost three times the value of the 17.2 million shares traded that day on the Sydney Stock Exchange. The SFE also enjoyed a record day in wool, which benefited from the generally heated trading. Some market observers expressed concern at the mounting interest in gold futures by novice and unsophisticated traders unfamiliar with the risks of a volatile futures market but eager for what looked like easy money. Some broking houses required private clients to lodge funds on deposit as a ready pool available to meet margin calls; the firms would allow a position to accumulate a specified amount in margin calls and then would close the client out. But not all clients appreciated such a cautious approach.

Responding to the market volatility, and anxious to avoid a situation where inexperienced traders could get into trouble, ICCH edged up the initial deposit on the SFE's gold contract.

When in October the deposit leaped by $500 to $2500, it was the fourth increase in a month, taking it to five times the value it had been when the gold contract opened in April 1978. At the same time, the SFE's solicitors provided the board with a letter reminding members of the exchange about standards of conduct and requesting that their advertisements refer only to services offered to the public and not make claims which could not be substantiated. There had been a rush of advertisements, some from SFE members and some not, making outlandish claims about the potential gains to be made in commodities trading. From around September 1979 the SFE began receiving letters of complaint from clients of floor and associate members. There was little the exchange could do, in the absence of rules under which it could force members, particularly associates, into line. But the board felt the pressures of those times, and meetings often lasted until midnight.

In the midst of chaotic trading in gold markets, the SFE launched its first interest-rate futures contract, based on a 90-day bank-accepted bill of exchange. The idea for such a contract had been sown some years earlier when it became clear that futures based on financial instruments had become dominant in the US, where enormous activity had built up in interest-rate futures based on Ginnie Maes and Fannie Maes and traded on the Chicago exchanges. Why not bring such a contract to Australia? Clive Hall, as chairman, welcomed Andy McConnel to a meeting of the currency consultative group on 6 September 1978 to discuss the introduction of a 90-day interest-rate contract. McConnel said such a contract would 'enable banks and merchant banks to gain valuable experience in futures trading . . . the market would provide a hedge for bill rollovers as well as for companies which need to make seasonal fund-raisings and also against seasonal tightening of liquidity and interest rates'. To the best of his knowledge it would not contravene any existing legislation; nor would it require Reserve Bank approval.

McConnel, who said that he and Desmond Brook did the 'hack work' to get interest-rate futures off the ground, also said that Clive Hall did a 'superb marketing job', canvassing the concept of interest-rate futures among the short-term money market and merchant banking fraternity. Vigorous activity in the gold contract had awakened the interest of the financial markets in the potential of futures, and they were receptive to early discussions about an interest-rate contract. A financial instruments committee was formed early in 1979, including McConnel (chairman), Bob Wright, David Greig, Gerry van Wyngen and Les Pegg, to examine what instrument would be most appropriate. The committee concluded that the proposed contract should be based on a 90-day bank-accepted bill—already enjoying a very healthy physical market—with bills suitable for delivery being only those accepted by one of the clearing banks. A major step in the contract's development was achieved with the agreement of the Commonwealth Bank to act as settlement agent. This had come about through the efforts of Gerry van Wyngen and Andy McConnel, in discussions initially with Kevin O'Donnell and then, after O'Donnell moved to BT Australia, with David Williams who succeeded O'Donnell as head of the Commonwealth Bank's money-market division. Williams took what was essentially a trading-bank matter to Stan Kelly, general manager of the Commonwealth Trading Bank, and, to the delight of the bill contract's promoters, secured a speedy agreement that the Commonwealth Bank would be settlement agent and vet the bills lodged for delivery to ensure they complied with the contract's specifications. Considerable work went into defining the bank's responsibilities. Having the Commonwealth Bank—a dominant force in the bill market—perform this role gave an important boost to the proposed contract.

ICCH and the bank began work on delivery procedures for the bill contract, with the team handling the project consisting of Les Hosking from ICCH and Phil Gray, Ed Condran and Jim Wheatley from the Commonwealth Bank. The financial instruments committee called a meeting in July 1979, inviting all floor members interested in bill futures to attend. 'That was the Clive Hall method,' said McConnel. 'You get people involved and revved up.'

The board decided at a meeting on 11 July 1979 to introduce a new classification of associate member—a full associate member—who would have the right to trade at associate members' brokerage rates on all markets of the SFE. Full associate membership would be offered from 1 August at $12 500. With gold sparking considerable activity, and an interest-rate futures contract on the horizon, enthusiasm for futures was heightening in the financial markets. The Commonwealth Bank, then an associate member of the SFE, took the view that futures offered worthwhile opportunities but the conservative bank was not about to jump into an unknown area without first satisfying itself that the move would be worthwhile. Phil Gray was given the task of researching the futures markets and, for about a year, he read as much as he could find about the operation of financial futures in the established US markets.

But late in 1979 events gathered momentum. Phil Gray recalled that Graham Parkhurst, then senior manager fixed interest and planning, expressed some concerns that David Williams would take the bank into futures before it was ready. 'You're worried he might dip his toe into the water?' queried Gray. 'No,' replied Parkhurst. 'I'm worried that he'll take a flying leap off the diving board.' Parkhurst was proved half-right when Williams announced in November 1979 that the Commonwealth Bank had just executed its first futures contract—in wool. Williams recounted how this came about:

> A branch manager of the bank rang from western NSW, where a stock-and-station agent had held a roadshow about the benefits of futures and this had prompted a local farmer—a very good client of the bank—to go into the bank and demand why it didn't offer futures trading to customers. So the branch manager rang me and demanded to know why the bank didn't do this. My response was: well, we have plenty of collateral, so we will. Otherwise we could lose a customer. And miss a deal.

A problem was that the Commonwealth Bank, while having the approval to trade futures, did not have the experience or even the basic documentation to carry out a wool futures trade. Williams rang Gerry van Wyngen, then at AML Finance Corporation (a floor member of the SFE), who obligingly sent over a blank contract note. Williams put a line through the name 'AML Finance Corporation Ltd', wrote 'Commonwealth Trading Bank', filled out the details of the trade and sent the note off to the customer as evidence of the transaction. Phil Gray, struck by the significance of the moment, took a copy of the contract note to the bank's archivist. 'One day the Commonwealth Bank will be a big force

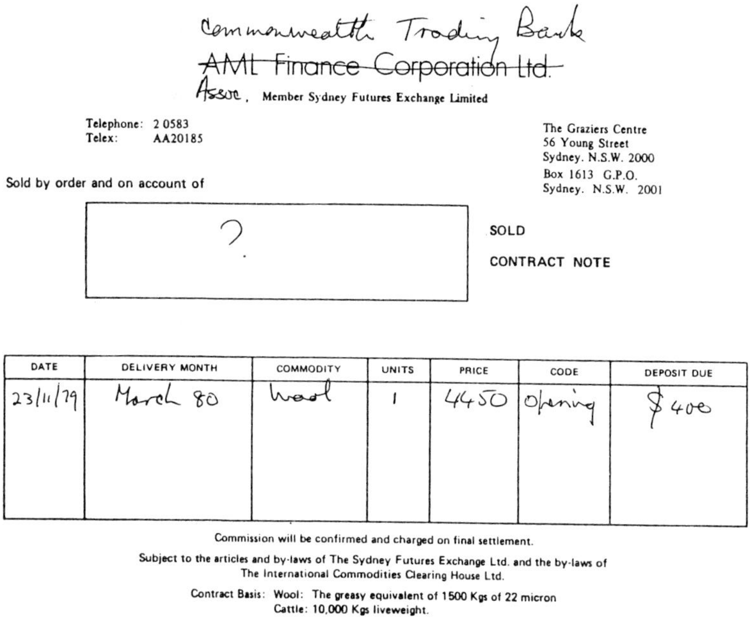

Commonwealth Trading Bank
~~AML Finance Corporation Ltd.~~
Assoc., Member Sydney Futures Exchange Limited

Telephone: 2 0583
Telex: AA20185

The Graziers Centre
56 Young Street
Sydney. N.S.W. 2000
Box 1613 G.P.O.
Sydney. N.S.W. 2001

Sold by order and on account of

?

SOLD

CONTRACT NOTE

DATE	DELIVERY MONTH	COMMODITY	UNITS	PRICE	CODE	DEPOSIT DUE
23/11/79	March 80	Wool	1	4450	Opening	$400

Commission will be confirmed and charged on final settlement.

Subject to the articles and by-laws of The Sydney Futures Exchange Ltd. and the by-laws of The International Commodities Clearing House Ltd.

Contract Basis: Wool: The greasy equivalent of 1500 Kgs of 22 micron
Cattle: 10,000 Kgs liveweight.

The contract note which signified the Commonwealth Bank's entry into futures trading. Phil Gray had the foresight to lodge it with the bank's archivist.

in the futures market and this contract note is where it all started,' he told the grateful archivist.

A second wave of financial institutions applied for membership of the SFE to trade the interest-rate futures contract—and triggered a bitter rift in the board. The board had recommended five new floor members—Bisley Commodities Pty Ltd, Merrill Lynch, Ord Minnett, Capel Court Corporation and Schroder Darling. The members rejected their applications. Hall, incensed, reminded them that they were trying to run an exchange, not a closed club, and that they had rejected names that included bluebloods in world merchant banking and broking circles.

At a board meeting a couple of days later, on 28 August 1979, an exasperated Hall said the results of the members' ballot were unbelievable. In his view, the failure of the floor members to elect applicants of such status represented a vote of no confidence in the board. He offered his resignation and suggested that all directors should resign and allow the members to re-elect the board. He left the meeting. Desmond Brook took the chair. The meeting decided to ask Hall to reconsider. Hall returned to the meeting but was adamant that he would not change his view and again left. Brook and McConnel were deputised to dissuade Hall from resigning but he stuck to his guns. Brook was elected chairman of the board and McConnel deputy chairman. Hall's resignation left one board seat vacant; he was invited to apply for that, which he did, and later that month again took a place on the board, as an ordinary member.

Meanwhile, some of the rejected group went public with a suggestion that they would form their own exchange with a number of other big players in the financial markets. According to *The Australian Financial Review*, 30 August 1979, they were acting not out of spite but because of a determination to get interest-rate and currency futures moving as soon as possible. The SFE was keen to have floor members reconsider their decision. For their part, the floor members said that their rejection of the proposed new members was not an attempt to restrict membership but a reflection of simple arithmetic: with twenty members, only six disapprovals were needed to block an application (each application needed two-thirds support to succeed). However, it was known that members were also concerned about staff resources which could be threatened by an increase in numbers.

Early in September the SFE floor members voted in the five they had previously rejected: Bisley, Merrill Lynch, Ord Minnett, Capel Court and Schroder Darling. They were the successes out of a list of nineteen applicants and their admission did not immediately defuse plans to form another exchange.

Interest-rate futures began trading on 17 October. A week later, the US prime rate rose to 15 per cent, and the new conservative government in the UK, under Prime Minister Margaret Thatcher, abandoned exchange controls. Activity was robust on the SFE but much of the financial and commodities markets' interest was occupied by revelations in the US of an attempt to corner the silver market and a move by the Chicago Board of Trade to force groups of traders to loosen their grip on silver futures. At the same time, Comex in New York took the unusual step of ensuring that small traders could not get into silver futures. For while gold had been hogging the headlines, silver was also staging an enormous surge in price, largely due to the activities of the brothers Nelson and Bunker Hunt and various Arab interests. Believing that silver was underpriced, they bought as much of the metal as possible, generating a huge amount of speculative activity that forced its price to $US50 an ounce. At one stage the Hunt consortium was said to control about half of the world's supply of silver. In the end, the Hunts failed to corner the market and sustained huge losses when the silver price crashed—plummeting to below $10 by the end of June 1980.

November 1979 opened with a downturn in the gold price and futures brokers were steering clients instead into wool and cattle. However, these markets were also fairly uncertain and within a few days the gold price had taken off again, on the back of a crisis in Iran that threatened the oil price. The SFE turned over 2033 gold contracts as traders who had shifted to other commodities resumed their activity. But the buoyancy was shortlived. The gold market settled and speculators turned to cattle and to the newly launched interest-rate futures contract, which was deriving considerable attention following an increase in the US prime rate to 15.75 per cent and a lift in the UK's minimum lending rate to 17 per cent.

By late November gold was trading only a few hundred contracts a day and commodity prices generally were down. But the nervousness had not entirely left the market and it would take only a whiff of crisis to reignite the panic. This occurred early in December. Gold prices soared when tension mounted in the Middle East, the US embassy in Libya was burned, riots broke out in Saudi Arabia and unrest intensified in Iran. Gold settled around $US425, then rose again in New York, Hong Kong and London to $US442. News in mid-December that Saudi Arabia, the United Arab Emirates and Qatar had increased oil prices ahead of the forthcoming OPEC meeting sent gold to $US455. In Sydney, the December contract hit $US485 and April $US518. On 27 December gold broke the $US500 barrier in New York, hitting $US510 on thin trading characteristic of the festive season. In London, gold closed the year at $US524.

At the end of 1979 the SFE could look back on a tumultuous year. It had been eventful almost from the start, with the first financial collapse of a floor member occurring in February when Booth Newman Pty Ltd was unable to meet its commitments to the clearing house. Booth Newman's problems involved a major client, the wool exporter Booth Hill and Sons (which was also a major shareholder in Booth Newman), double options in wool and an unexpectedly large rise in the wool price that left Booth Hill unable to pay on the day the necessary deposits and margin calls.

Dick Newman, who had been in the futures industry since joining W.P. Martin Whittingham Pty Ltd, a founding member of the exchange, was a one-time chairman of the SFE board and still a board member in 1979 when his company went down. Newman had felt slightly apprehensive about the direction of the wool price during February 1979. He knew that Booth Hill and Sons had granted hundreds of double options in wool. These involved substantial risk for the grantor because the options could be exercised by those who had taken either puts (options to sell) or calls (options to buy); however, the grantor stood to make healthy profits from the double premiums paid by the takers of the options. Booth Hill had considerable experience in granting double options. Newman, a fourth-generation wooltrader and managing director of Booth Newman since it began trading in February 1964, was conscious that the wool price had been rising for some three weeks on the back of enthusiastic Japanese buying orders. Booth Hill had covered itself against the risk of a price fall by selling forward in the futures market. When Booth Hill granted the options the wool price was around 365 cents a kilogram and most of the options had a strike price of 370 cents (that was the price at which the futures contracts would have to be written if the options were exercised). Booth Hill was banking on a fall in the wool price.

As the wool price rose, the firm had to adjust its position by taking bought contracts to offset its contracts to sell. By mid-February wool had hit Booth Hill's strike price of 370 cents and a week later, on 23 February, the price leapt 41 cents a kilogram to 411 cents, representing for Booth Hill a paper loss of $615 for each futures contract. The speed of this unexpected rise left Booth Hill unable to cover its sold contracts or to open new bought contracts. At the close of trading on Friday 23 February the company faced margin calls amounting to hundreds of thousands of dollars. Hopes that Monday's trading would see the price subside were unfulfilled; instead the disaster was compounded as the wool futures price climbed to 440 cents a kilogram, increasing Booth Hill's liabilities on each contract to $1050. Worried by the swift moves, the clearing house doubled the deposits on option contracts to $400. Booth Hill informed its broker, Booth Newman, that it could not meet the additional deposits and margin calls. Booth Newman, responsible as floor member for payment of the calls to ICCH, could not produce the required sum by the 2.30pm deadline on the following day. On 27 February Dick Newman sent a letter to clients:

> This company has been prevented by events beyond its control from meeting the requirements of the Clearing House and has ceased to trade today at 2.30pm, when the ultimate default of a major client led to the ascertainment of this position.

The clearing house entered the market that afternoon and bought Booth Newman's net short positions. At a board meeting on 7 March, it was confirmed that although the outstanding wool contracts of Booth Newman had not been closed out, the clearing house now held contracts which, if matched out, would bring the open position of Booth Newman in wool almost to zero. Nigel Mainwaring, from the law firm Laurence & Laurence, explained the board's choice: either to suspend Booth Newman and recommend to members that it be expelled, or allow the company time to meet the clearing house requirements for solvency and then decide on a course of action.

The board resolved to debar Booth Newman from trading until further notice. The client, Booth Hill, which had been an associate member since the exchange began in 1960, was advised that it was to be expelled. Booth Hill wrote to the SFE to object, saying 'expulsion rather than suspension is an unduly harsh penalty to be imposed . . . at this stage'. Booth Hill continued:

> . . . whilst it is your right under your Articles of Association to expel us, your decision appears premature in light of the

> delays we have experienced, and unnecessarily harsh in light of our past record and in light of the circumstances surrounding that period, not only market movement but the final action by International Commodities Clearing House Limited of doubling the deposits at such short notice.

Within a few months Booth Hill had fully reimbursed Booth Newman. Booth Hill was wound up and its assets bought by Farmers and Graziers Cooperative Ltd. Booth Newman's membership was subsequently bought by the large pastoral house Elder Smith Goldsborough Mort Ltd and, managed by Dick Newman, began trading again on the SFE on 6 June. No-one has traded double options on the SFE since Booth Newman defaulted.

Gold had become the focus of the SFE during 1979 and the exchange had taken a giant leap forward in terms of public profile. Twelve months earlier few outside the industry had known much about commodity futures; by the end of 1979 a vast proportion of the general public had dabbled in gold futures. This was the SFE's first exposure to traders who were not 'professionals', and it came at a time when there were no regulations covering dealings with the public. Most brokers operated on the principle that so long as deposits and margins were called from clients everything was in order. Some brought trouble on themselves through a lack of vigilance in calling margins, a discipline that often played second fiddle in the rush to write new business and earn commissions. The exchange's articles and by-laws covered the conduct of floor members when trading in SFE markets but did not regulate the relationships between floor members and their clients. There was no provision in the rules for settlement or arbitration of disputes between a member and a client, although in certain conditions the SFE could arbitrate in disputes between members of the exchange. A consequence of bringing in brokers as floor members, and the resultant involvement of the wider public, was a greater interest taken in the SFE's business by regulators such as the Corporate Affairs Commission and the Trade Practices Commission. The SFE, managing unprecedented market activity with a set of rules drafted twenty years earlier for a wool futures market, began working on new regulations which would require stricter financial control and generally higher standards of conduct from members dealing with the public. The new discipline emphasised self-regulation and was designed to lift the public's confidence in the futures industry.

The NSW government, too, was interested—largely through its role in discussions relating to the cash-settled currency contracts and the implications for them of the Gaming and Betting Act. The Futures Market Bill was introduced in the NSW parliament in December 1979. The SFE board met to discuss the possible ramifications and deputised Desmond Brook, Andy McConnel, Pat Nicholas, Nigel Mainwaring of Laurence & Laurence and Jim Sinclair from ICCH to discuss amendments to the proposed legislation with the Corporate Affairs Commission. The Act brought the articles and by-laws of the SFE and ICCH under the control of the NSW Attorney-General, and changes to business rules could be made only with the minister's agreement.

New contracts and expanded trading volumes meant that the SFE soon outgrew its premises in Australia Square and, on 20 July 1979, it moved to new headquarters at 13–15 O'Connell Street, diagonally opposite the building where it had been born in a small room almost twenty years earlier. Clive Hall had been negotiating for the SFE to move into Kindersley House in O'Connell Street, recently vacated by the Sydney Stock Exchange, which had moved to smart new premises at 20 Bond Street. When that did not eventuate, the SFE considered a site at the corner of Martin Place and George Street, an ANZ building at the time, which had a big banking chamber. That did not work out. Then Hall found 13–15 O'Connell Street. Trading in the new building began on Monday 23 July, after a dummy run on the previous Saturday. Preparations included getting ready for the introduction of digital clocks. The new premises of 8216 square feet were almost four times the size of the exchange's original home.

Towards the end of 1979 the exchange underwent changes in its small full-time staff. John Hooton, public relations officer, resigned on 21 December and Barry Thornley, the live cattle technical officer, also announced his intention to leave. Coincidentally, on 31 December, Desmond Brook received a letter from Andy McConnel informing him that McConnel was severing his connections with Ross McConnel Kitchen as of that date and that as a result would be resigning as a director of the SFE. The board recorded its appreciation of his contribution as a director and Brook, then chairman, moved that McConnel be appointed general manager of the SFE with authority over staffing arrangements. The appointment took effect from 14 January 1980. McConnel persuaded Thornley to stay with the SFE.

As the allure of gold trading spread through the Australian community in 1979, the firm Robert Howes & Associates, floor members of the SFE since February 1976, was regularly placing eye-catching advertisements pushing its services. Slogans such as 'This trading desk sees one in five futures contracts in Australia' and 'If you've just started to think about investing in gold, it's time to have a quiet word with the professionals' were designed to appeal to a public easily seduced by the promise of effortless profits. Howes, at one stage billed as 'Mr Commodities', was one of the brassiest brokers in the ranks of SFE membership. He had started in the commodities business in Perth in 1971 after a career that included stints as a real estate salesman, furniture retailer and dancing instructor. In 1975 Howes moved his business to Sydney and in the following year became a floor member of the SFE. The company embarked on a widespread publicity campaign, promoting commodities, particularly gold, and providing free investment seminars to a hungry public. As Colleen Ryan was to write in *The National Times* in May 1986:

> Howes' breakthrough—the secret of his success—was to bring futures trading and investment in gold bullion and diamonds to the attention of the ordinary Australian. Saturation advertising in the financial press, adept use of direct mail and free seminars all helped to spread the message. The Robert Howes image was a comfortable one for the small investor. There was no feeling of intimidation. Vinyl coats and fun fur were more the thing at a Howes seminar in the late seventies than leather and mink. Retirees and widows with lump sums studded the Howes client list.

The charismatic Howes won huge loyalty from his 165 staff, whom he looked after well with performance-oriented bonuses, regular extravagant cocktail parties and a free lunch delivered daily to each person's desk. In December 1979 Howes sold his interest in the company to two of his senior executives, Graham and Michael Oades, who changed the firm's name to the Darlington Group. From May 1980, the company traded as Darlington Commodities Ltd. Darlington promoted itself as active in commodity futures and options, bullion dealing and investment diamonds. Its claims were far from modest. One advertisement boasted: 'Thanks to Darlington I made over 264% profit on one diamond—another Darlington case history.' Under Michael Oades, Darlington introduced managed futures accounts, where trading was handled on behalf of clients at the manager's discretion, for a minimum investment of $10 000. Darlington's ambitious diversification led it to set up a rural division and later, in July 1981, it became the Australian representative of the prestige broking firm E.F. Hutton, then ranked third largest in the world. The Darlington group operated with some 40 companies under its banner, including Bullion Sales International Pty Ltd. In May 1984 Darlington Commodities Ltd transferred its bullion trading and storage activities—and several million dollars of debt—to Bullion Sales International Ltd, for $1. At the time, Michael Oades was a director of both companies. Darlington Commodities and Bullion Sales International were supposedly in the business of selling bullion and coins to the public, and storing bullion and coins for clients. Clients did not see their investments but received a receipt as security. It subsequently became evident that the companies did not acquire sufficient stock to cover the bullion sold to clients and purportedly stored on their behalf. Bullion Sales International collapsed in 1986 with debts of $5.5 million. Darlington was wound up in December of that year. Graham Oades went to live in England. Michael Oades was charged with numerous counts of cheating and defrauding investors and failing to act honestly as a director. In December 1988 he received a four-and-a-half-year jail sentence.

After the split with Oades, Robert Howes went on to concentrate on Alpex Commodity Traders, listed on the Sydney Stock Exchange, using the same flamboyant style to build up that company before its short but eventful life ended in 1981. A popular Alpex advertisement ran: 'If your money is in the bank you're going broke'. Howes, who featured prominently in the Alpex publicity, referred to his operation as 'your investment multiplier'.

The seductive advertisements run by Howes, Darlington and others, many of whom were not members of the SFE, were a constant worry to the exchange, with their wild promises of easy profits from trading gold on small deposits, and 'guaranteed' returns. Howes went on to deluge the public with advertisements; early in 1980, when he was managing director of Alpex Commodity Traders, he promised to show investors 'How to make $160 000 in nine months trading commodity futures'. Bargold Pty Ltd and Southern Cross Coins, neither of which was a member of the SFE, were also regularly advertising the advantages of buying gold.

During late 1979 and early 1980 commodities were hugely popular and their prices reflected this. Iron ore, lead and aluminium prices were up; copper hit record highs; sugar, tin, gold, silver, wool, nickel, rutile, steaming coal, diamonds, platinum, wheat, cotton, rubber and cobalt all rose. Many were later to fall spectacularly.

Meanwhile, 1980 opened with central banks and governments concerned about the frenzy in the gold market. A year earlier the gold price had been $US225 an ounce; now it was more than double that level, suggesting a lack of confidence in the international monetary system. The rise in the gold price prompted Paul Volcker, chairman of the US Federal Reserve, to warn that the frantic market for gold contained elements of a classic boom-bust: there were more speculators than the supply of speculative gold could satisfy. Gold rose in price as he spoke, reaching $US650 in Zurich on 3 January, after an opening level of $US610. Trading in London reached fever-pitch, with spreads as wide as $US30, and was suspended. The SFE traded a new record of 3286 contracts, mostly in the April contract. On Monday 7 January the gold price reached $US680 in Hong Kong, but in uncertain trading where the rise was not sustained. In Sydney, the SFE recorded another bumper day of 3071 trades in which a nervous market saw the April gold contract hit $US600. On Thursday 17 January *The Australian Financial Review* carried a headline 'Gold's Dizzy Day' and reported that gold had soared the day before to $US720 an ounce on a combination of war panic, official inaction and boom-time greed. For a few days the frenzy subsided, as though gathering strength for a final assault. On 21 January unprecedented buying demand sent the gold price rocketing to $US823/33 in Hong Kong; in Sydney the entry cost to the gold futures market was lifted to $12 000. *The Australian Financial Review* quoted a broker: 'If you can't afford $12 000, you shouldn't be in this market.'

On 23 January the bubble burst. Gold fell in chaotic trading, losing $US200 in one day; on the SFE the April gold contract was quoted at $US568. By the time the gold price crashed many people had made enormous fortunes and many others had lost amounts that left them shattered. Speculators and brokers alike suffered disastrous losses. In the year to January 1980, the movement of the gold price had defied logic and expectations, rising by 270 per cent from $US230 to $US850 an ounce. It then fell to $US474, down 45 per cent from its peak. Not only had the price rocketed at times, but intraday price jumps were common. For a precious metal whose price had been fixed for almost 40 years, such volatility was almost beyond belief. The prosperity that came with the boom was illustrated by the nonchalance with which SFE traders double-parked their Ferraris and Porsches in the street outside the exchange, content to pay fines rather than take the time to find a parking spot.

As the gold price crashed, it took a leading SFE floor member, Ross McConnel Kitchen, with it. On 13 February, RMK was suspended from trading at its own request. RMK had not defaulted to ICCH in terms of meeting its margins and deposits; rather, the firm's problems arose because of some $1 million owed to it by futures clients following the hectic trading of 23 January when the gold price plummeted worldwide. The directors decided that, in the light of this, the firm was technically insolvent. In a subsequent rescue, several clients converted what was owed to them into equity, injecting $1.2 million into RMK. The firm resumed trading on 15 February.

By May 1980 gold was at its quietest level in eighteen months. In the following month, unconfirmed rumours that US hostages in Iran had been shot sent the gold price up and in July the precious metal hit its highest level in three months. By September gold was staging a major rally, buoyed by renewed buying interest and speculation that another OPEC oil-price rise was coming. Estimates that the gold price could break above $US700 proved correct on 23 September, the first time gold had hit such a height since February. Trading was frantic on the SFE. Renewed interest in gold cash-and-carry brought a record number of 1090 deliveries in September on the SFE. By late 1980, president-elect Ronald Reagan had stated his intention to support the $US with high interest rates and gold came under selling pressure as US interest rates rose. By early 1981 the gold price was fragile and the metal, in common with other commodities that year, fell victim to the twin pressures of high interest rates and a recession.

The year 1980 has been remembered as the time of the speculator on world commodity markets, particularly in the highly volatile gold and silver markets. It was also the best year so far for the SFE, mostly because of the soaring gold price which drew in many first-time traders. Boom trading conditions resulted in trading volumes more than doubling to 611 270 compared with 265 380 in 1979. Gold was the most active, trading 229 846 contracts (more than double 1979's level), but had strong competition from live cattle and wool and, increasingly, the 90-day bank-accepted bill contract. The SFE recorded a number of milestones in 1980: the exchange turned twenty years old, and could celebrate by having traded its two millionth contract in May (it had reached its first million in 1974). Turnover hit record daily volumes in each market. And a new trading floor with the latest electronic video facilities had been opened in March when the then treasurer, John Howard, launched the currency futures contracts.

Interest in gold revived in mid-1981, with widespread expectations that its price could top the earlier peak of $US850. Several firms were advertising regularly, pushing the advantages of buying gold. The high-profile Darlington Commodities Limited used well-known names such as leading fashion designer Carla Zampatti (1980 Business Woman of the Year) and Bob Ansett, managing director of Budget Rent-A-Car, to promote its managed accounts in a splashy series of advertisements in February 1981. Managed accounts, said to suit traders too busy with their own business to keep up with the market day-by-day, were also offered by Robert Howes' vehicle, Alpex Commodity Traders.

In February 1981 Howes, an associate member of the SFE, was trying to regain floor membership of the exchange. He told *The Australian Financial Review* (27 February 1981) that he had 'done quite a bit for the futures industry'. 'When I was trading, my aim was to involve the public as much as possible with education programs,' he said. The following month, Alpex Commodity Traders announced its plans to establish a new property futures exchange in Sydney, to be structured to enable the small investor to climb on the bandwagon of the prevailing property boom. The promotion of the proposed venture was in typically flamboyant Howes style, with glossy brochures and glittering media events to spread the word. However, Alpex was forced to modify its plans after talks with the Queensland and NSW Corporate Affairs Commissions. Then, in October, an Alpex subsidiary, T.C. Moritz Holdings Pty Ltd, defaulted on a $3.5 million loan from Citicorp Australia Holdings Ltd. Citicorp appointed receivers and managers to take over T.C. Moritz's Monte Carlo home unit project on the Gold Coast—the first venture set up to trade on Alpex's proposed property futures exchange. At the end of the month Alpex reported a loss of $2.5 million for 1980/81. Early in November the SFE debarred Alpex from trading as an associate member until it had settled with all its creditors. A receiver was appointed to Alpex on 11 November. The receiver described the administration of the company as 'unbelievably deplorable'; transactions executed in September had not been fed into the computer until November. In December 1981 Alpex's office furniture and assets were auctioned; the catalogue included a gold-coloured Rolls Royce, an antique English mahogany boardroom table and other leather-and-walnut furniture.

Overall, 1981 was a shaky year for the SFE. A number of firms collapsed, including Alpex and Sydney Metal Exchange Pty Ltd. In April 1981 the SFE suspended the insolvent Burchell and Walsh Futures Pty Ltd, which specialised in rural commodities. The company was wound up. These casualties came on top of the winding-up in 1980 of two associate members, Gibraltar Services Pty Ltd of Mildura and Commodity Brokers of Australia Pty Ltd. The failures highlighted the inadequacy of rules which gave the SFE no authority over associate members, a fact that the exchange was finding increasingly disturbing in view of the financial difficulties hitting some of the almost-400 associate members. The collapses made headlines, and did nothing for the SFE's public image.

An ebullient advertisement announced Robert Howes' comeback in 1982: 'Splendid news. Robert Howes is back! The man who put commodities on the map in Australia is back in business . . .' An article in *The Australian Financial Review*, headlined 'Robert Howes does a Lazarus', reported:

> Robert Howes, the commodity futures broker who rode the gold and property booms until the latter bit him, is attempting a comeback. Barely six month after his Alpex Commodity Traders Ltd went into receivership and with its final position still unclear—at last report it will be lucky to meet its debts of about $22 million—Mr Howes is striking out on his own.
>
> He has leased a luxury unit in Sydney's fashionable Broughton House in Clarence Street and has adventurous plans to re-establish himself in the commodity industry . . . And during a frank interview . . . Mr Howes was excited and enthusiastic about his comeback plans. 'I suppose it was a bit of a cheek, the type of advertisement I put in,' he confessed. 'But then I thought if I don't blow my own trumpet, nobody else will.'

The paper reported that spokesmen for the receiver and the NSW Corporate Affairs Commission expressed surprise that Howes was back in business, but both said that there was nothing to stop him. Howes worked as senior consultant to Central Commodities Services Pty Ltd, a company 80 per cent owned by his wife Jean and daughter Sally which, despite a Reserve Bank regulation prohibiting speculation on overseas futures markets, operated a number of managed funds specialising in overseas markets and provided a 24-hour service to clients. In June 1983 Howes sold his family's interest in the business and a couple of months later he left Australia. By the time the receivers were brought into Central Commodities the new owners had also gone, leaving a shortfall of several million dollars.

Robert Howes, the high-roller who had brought the spotlight on to commodity futures trading, with mixed results and probably to the detriment of the Sydney Futures Exchange, was last seen in Australia in September 1983. He and his family fled overseas, to Hong Kong, the US and then England, eluding the authorities along the way. Hard on Howes' trail have been the NSW Corporate Affairs Commission, the Victorian branch of the Federal Director of Public Prosecutions and Interpol. The CAC has 81 warrants for his arrest on charges arising from investigations into Alpex, including conspiracy to cheat and defraud, obtaining financial advantage by deception and cheating and defrauding under the Crimes Act. Over the years Howes has used a number of assumed names and numerous bank accounts in Hong Kong, Luxembourg, the US and UK. In 1989 a former director of Alpex Commodity Traders Pty Ltd, Bruce Murphy, was sentenced to eight years' jail with a non-parole period of five years after being found guilty of nineteen criminal charges.

4
Playing by the rules

The Sydney Futures Exchange struggled for the first few months of 1980 to shake off the consequences of the gold boom-and-bust. The gold price had collapsed on 23 January, ending a phase in gold futures markets that had brought drama, notoriety and lingering problems. Casualties of the gold era included members and associate members of the exchange, as well as individuals who had traded the markets. Andy McConnel, at that time general manager of the SFE, was fielding a number of complaints from these individual traders. A key source of financial problems for members had been their neglect, or reluctance, to call margins from clients. Floor members had to pay margins to ICCH, but there was an element of discretion among some in calling margins from clients. Writing business and generating commissions was paramount in those heady days.

In May 1980 the SFE appointed its first chief executive, Dr David Rutledge. Until that point the SFE had operated with a board, which was virtually a management committee making all decisions, and a succession of general managers. The chairman operated almost as an extension of the exchange's staff (this relationship became more formal as the 1980s progressed). ICCH had a big influence over the operations of the futures market. With the appointment of a chief executive, the board, frequently criticised for not delegating,

David Rutledge, chief executive of the Sydney Futures Exchange from 1980 to the end of 1984.

for the first time had someone to whom it could devolve authority. Rutledge's interest in futures had developed while he was studying at the Food Research Institute of Stanford University under Professor Roger Gray—whom Clive Hall had brought to Australia in 1966 to review the SGWFE's operations and lecture about the futures industry. Rutledge had completed his doctoral thesis on 'The relationship between price and hedging patterns in the US soybean complex'. His work experience included two years with a major grain company in New York, Continental Grain, as well as several years in academia, first at Macquarie University in

Sydney and then at Stanford. When, in 1978, the world's largest metals futures exchange, Commodity Exchange Inc of New York (Comex), was looking to appoint an economist with futures industry connections he grabbed the chance, becoming a senior vice-president of what was then the third-largest futures exchange in the US.

By August 1979 Rutledge was considering returning, with his wife Annemarie and two young children, to Australia and possibly to a post with Macquarie University. He had already been associated with the SFE on several occasions as a consultant, having met Clive Hall previously through Roger Gray. He wrote to Hall, advising him of his plans. Hall rang Rutledge in New York, expressing enthusiasm for a renewed involvement with the SFE. In February 1980 Rutledge was again appointed as a consultant to the exchange and then, in May, to the position of chief executive officer. A press release issued by the SFE said he would be 'responsible to the board of directors for all aspects of the exchange's operations' and that the general manager, Andy McConnel, would 'report to Dr Rutledge and take responsibility for managing the exchange on a day-to-day basis'.

McConnel left the exchange in September 1980. His departure came at a time when his principal task of installing a management structure was virtually completed, but he was also under board pressure to resign. He rejected suggestions that he had been asked to go because of litigation involving SFE floor member RMK, of which he had formerly been a partner. He pointed out that when RMK's problems had arisen earlier in the year he had offered to resign but the board had seen no need. McConnel said his departure was over a 'personal matter' between him and the board. During his time in the job McConnel had hired, among others, Barry Grant as floor manager and Stephen Calder to handle public relations. Calder's appointment followed the departure of John Hooton, who had been the exchange's public relations manager since 1975. A former journalist with *The Australian*, Calder had specialised in futures and co-authored a book on the subject, *Futures Stock*. When he joined the SFE in April 1980 it operated with a staff of twenty; by the time he left, ten years later, staff numbers had risen to around 140.

Rutledge, having come from Comex, a successful major

international market, brought a degree of credibility that boosted the SFE's stature. Further, his earlier role as an academic observer of the futures industry suggested that he was able to discuss futures objectively—to demonstrate that they performed a useful function in the business and financial system. 'The whole concept of projecting the SFE as a credible institution in 1980 was a challenge,' Rutledge said. 'And that applied in dealings with government as well as with the broad community.' Stephen Calder handled press communications while Rutledge threw himself into a series of public speaking engagements, addressing a range of audiences from lawyers to exporters around Australia, talking to everyone he could, spreading the word about the SFE.

The SFE had no surplus income in those years but was keen to expand, develop new products and improve facilities. Potential markets in fat lambs, coal and copper were considered. Rutledge told *The Australian* (23 June 1980): 'We are going through a period of consolidation after the rapid growth in the market and we are looking to ensuring we have a well-organised and well-trained staff.' His opinion was that further growth was most likely in financial futures.

The exchange enjoyed good levels of business during 1980 with trading activity up 131 per cent over 1979, stretching facilities and staff. Turnover in wool soared in February, and in late March the six-month-old 90-day bank-accepted bill futures contract broke records when it traded 160 lots in one day. Gold enjoyed a resurgence in September, with renewed tension in the Middle East reviving buying interest; frantic trading late in September saw the gold price above $US700 for the first time since February. Of a total of 611 268 contracts traded in 1980 gold took the lion's share, accounting for 229 846 and notching up a daily average of 905 contracts. Live cattle was the next busiest contract, turning in its fifth successive record year with 184 214 contracts traded, compared with 49 937 the previous year. Trading in wool more than doubled 1979's levels: 173 308 contracts changed hands, with a daily average volume of 684. The SFE could report an after-tax surplus of $42 007, a substantial turnaround from the previous year's deficit of $3911. The SFE ended 1980 buoyed by its foray into financial instruments and preparing for further expansion. Even before the year was out it was clear that the

Clive Hall (right) initiates Doug Anthony, leader of the Country Party, into the mysteries of futures trading after the launch of the fat lamb contract in July 1981.

twenty-year-old exchange had already outgrown its new home. The exchange had spent $600 000 moving from Australia Square, where it had operated for ten years, and the new O'Connell Street premises had doubled the available space. Clearly, that was not going to be enough.

The record levels of activity enjoyed during 1980, though, were not repeated in 1981. Two new contracts launched in that year, silver and fat lambs, were not successful. As Rutledge commented in the annual report, 1981 was in many ways a difficult year for the exchange. Trading volumes were disappointingly low, dropping 26 per cent from the admittedly buoyant levels of the previous year. Within that, though, the 90-day bank-accepted bill futures contract recorded a 66 per cent rise in volume, $US futures rose and live cattle futures struck yet another record turnover. Poor performances came from gold and wool, both suffering from an absence of volatility and the generally low level of interest displayed in commodity markets worldwide. Gold, where activity fell by almost 46 per cent, traded in a narrow price range compared with the dramatic highs and lows of 1980. Wool activity was dampened by a historically high floor price which reduced the downside risk and so curtailed interest in hedging. Yen futures, launched in March 1980, and frozen boneless beef, introduced in April 1979, were suspended early in 1981, both having attracted minimal interest. During 1981 the exchange nonetheless made several achievements. Considerable progress was made in improving standards of self-regulation. A representative office was established in Melbourne, an office for the clearing house was also opened in the Victorian capital, and a bill settlement facility was introduced, all of which reinforced the national nature of the exchange.

A major issue confronting the SFE during 1981 was its image, which was suffering from bouts of unfavourable publicity that left it tagged 'a casino for speculators'. To help rectify this negative perception, the SFE's articles and by-laws were to be revamped. The exchange's rules mostly dated from its inception in 1960, although several significant amendments had been made in the intervening years. The exchange operated much like an old-fashioned businessmen's club, dealing with members and clients on the apparent assumption that all were gentlemen and that any breaches of good practice were mere accidents. Within a few months of the passage of the NSW Futures Markets Act in 1979 the NSW Corporate Affairs Commission had made it known that this was an optimistic assumption. The act gave the CAC power of supervision over the SFE's rules. The CAC did not insist on any immediate amendments to the rules but said they would have to be thoroughly overhauled in due course. Some senior members of the exchange dragged the chain, forcing Rutledge into the role of whip-cracker during 1980 and 1981.

In Rutledge's view, the articles had to be rewritten to win government approval. An articles and by-laws committee was established, under the chairmanship of Desmond Brook and including Dick Newman, David Rutledge and Les Hosking (then with ICCH). The committee worked with the SFE's legal advisers, Laurence & Laurence, to revise completely the SFE's articles and by-laws. The job made huge demands on time and negotiating skills. 'There were divisions among those in the subcommittee,' Rutledge says, 'with Desmond and Dick reluctant to approve significant change and very influenced by the UK model, whereas I was influenced by what I had seen in the US.' The new articles and by-laws recognised the structural changes which had occurred in the Australian futures industry during the previous few years and, in particular, embodied a degree of protection for the general public that was absent from the existing regulations. Rutledge later described the changes as having 'perhaps the most far-reaching ramifications for the industry'. While there have been significant changes since, the structure and principles set down then remain as a definition of the Australian futures markets.

The adoption by floor members of the exchange's new articles and by-laws took effect from February 1982. One of the rules entrenched the requirement that floor members must call for margins. Another allowed holders of futures positions to exchange them for the physical commodity, provided certain conditions were met; thus exchange-for-physical (EFP), providing additional flexibility for hedgers, was created. Rutledge commented in the annual report:

> The new regulations were the result of protracted discussions with the NSW Corporate Affairs Commission and long hours of work by the Articles and By-laws committee whose aim was to provide a self-regulatory framework which provided adequate protection to the general public and at the same time allowed traditional commercial practice in the industry to continue. It gives me some satisfaction to report that I believe these aims have been met . . .

The new rules vastly improved the SFE's self-regulation and provided far greater protection for members of the public. They placed special obligations on all members dealing with the public, clarified the rights and obligations of members to each other and to their clients and created a committee of inspection and audit with the wide-ranging power to examine members' records and check on margins and deposits. Members had to operate with a stipulated level of financial backing and had to submit quarterly reports on their financial position. Margin-calling became compulsory, not a matter of discretion between broker and client (it had always been compulsory between the clearing house and an exchange member). Clients' funds were to be properly placed.

Included in the new rules was a provision that the board of the exchange should include two independent directors who would provide objective assessments and help deal with potential conflicts of interest of other board members. This was a prescient move, given the importance that was to be given a few years later to the role of independent directors on corporate boards generally. It was a measure that considerably enhanced the stature of the SFE. The two independent directors appointed were Frank Ryan, a former chairman of the NSW Corporate Affairs Commission, and John Oliver, a former chairman and president of the Rural Bank of NSW (now State Bank NSW) and a subsequent chairman of the SFE. The appointment of Ryan and Oliver to the board filled the positions left vacant by the retirement of Clive Hall and the resignation of Greg Dodds. Together with chief executive David Rutledge, the two independent directors formed the new committee of inspection and audit (CIA), established to scrutinise the activities of members and ensure they complied with the SFE rules. Hall was succeeded as chairman by Phil Gardiner, a director of Hill Samuel Australia Ltd (now Macquarie Bank). Desmond Brook became deputy chairman. Oliver took strengthening the board a stage further when he requested that the chief executive of the SFE be included on the board, a move that provided the chief executive with a voting as well as advisory role and improved the balance of a board comprising five floor-member directors, two associate member directors and two independents.

The new articles and by-laws undoubtedly put the SFE on a far sounder footing but Rutledge and the board were conscious of one flaw—that non-members of the exchange were not subject to the restrictions, financial safeguards and behavioural code now rigorously imposed on floor and associate members. Rutledge wrote in the annual report: 'Certain activities of non-members, and in particular the forms of public advertisement adopted by some self-styled commodity trading firms outside the exchange's ambit, are a source of continuing concern to the exchange.' Southern Cross Commodities, a commodities trading firm incorporated in Adelaide in October 1980, with a penchant for eye-catching advertisements promising easy profits, was one of the non-members Rutledge had in mind.

Futures trading, with its highly speculative nature and low entry fee, has often attracted undesirable participants ready to exploit the unwary. The SFE had constantly had to be on guard in an effort to maintain standards in the industry. The early 1980s were a particularly trying time and while the worst excesses of 'bucket shops'—fringe operators which ostensibly invested clients' funds on foreign markets but often retained the funds themselves—were not apparent until a few years later, there were some earlier examples. Bucket shops would pay 'winnings' to a client if the market showed a profit on the client's investment; if the market moved against the client, the broker pocketed the funds. Orders were telexed overseas to create an illusion of execution. These operators often advertised widely, making misleading promises of big profits, but did not make plain that they were not members of the SFE and were not bound by the SFE's rules and code of behaviour. The state corporate affairs commissions, as well as federal and state police, investigated a number of such operations.

The SFE had received several complaints from members of the public about the trading practices of Southern Cross. The exchange did not like the company's business methods, nor its style of advertising. In due course, Rutledge learned that the South Australian Corporate Affairs Commission had started an investigation into Southern Cross. During the second half of 1982 a problem emerged, involving Southern Cross, that was to pose a potentially serious threat to the exchange. Despite SFE safeguards against unwelcome market participants, Southern Cross came close to claiming membership of the exchange when it found a willing seller of a business that included an existing floor membership. Southern Cross engaged in an intricate series of arm's-length negotiations with Simonius Pty Ltd, the Australian arm of the respected Swiss-based wool and commodities broking firm Simonius Vischer. Simonius Vischer, a founding member of the SFE, wished to get out of the wool business in Australia and New Zealand and sought a new shareholder for Simonius Pty Ltd. For Simonius Pty Ltd, Southern Cross offered a widespread client list; for Southern Cross, the deal offered a way into the SFE. Simonius Pty Ltd's strategy was to have Southern Cross operate as its sales organisation while Simonius, backed by its strong name and track record, would oversee trading activities.

The SFE, already perturbed that interests associated with Southern Cross were emerging as the buyers of a floor member—changes for which the necessary approval of the SFE membership had been neither sought nor given—was provided with a further distraction when Simonius Pty Ltd filed its June 1982 quarterly financial returns, showing the company was in breach of the rule requiring a minimum $100 000 net tangible assets. Simonius was given a few days to remedy this but could not do so, citing a 'transitory stage' pending a change in shareholder. Simonius was suspended from trading.

Rutledge's worries came to a head when it was discovered that, following a series of complex, connected deals, control of Simonius Pty Ltd had fallen into the hands of Southern Cross. The new owners fired the small staff of Simonius and replaced the existing directors. Rutledge's chief concern was that clients of Simonius Pty Ltd should not lose money as a result of the changes; he was also anxious that any transfer of a membership placed it in strong hands acceptable to the exchange and its members. Rutledge recalls what followed as 'one of his most important initiatives while at the SFE': he demanded Simonius' client list and arranged for all of the clients, and those of Southern Cross who had shifted their business to Simonius, either to have their open positions transferred to another floor member or their balances paid out.

The management of Southern Cross claimed that certain clients were happy to leave their funds in Southern Cross. Rutledge took the precaution of ringing them to hear for himself that they were happy to stay with Southern Cross. Working with James Williams of Laurence & Laurence, Rutledge reviewed the list of Simonius' clients and ensured that any amounts owed to them were paid out or transferred. Under pressure from Rutledge, Simonius' clients were paid out by bank cheque. Rutledge handled the distribution and mailing of the cheques, personally posting them from the Sydney GPO. No client of Simonius lost money. The episode would have been enormously damaging had it been widely known, said Rutledge. 'As it was, there was much harm done to the futures industry generally by the revelations of Southern Cross's activities,' he said. Simonius' seat on the SFE was subsequently bought by Wardley Australia Commodities Ltd.

Rutledge was under enormous personal pressure during the weekend before finally tidying up the clients' accounts. 'I'd taken the family up to Desmond Brook's farm at Wyong for the weekend, and felt truly ill driving back to Sydney on the Sunday evening,' he said. 'No one else knew exactly what was happening. Some of the board members didn't realise just how much even the appearance of a relationship with Southern Cross could damage the SFE.' Rutledge had known he was in a race against time: he was aware that a ten-month investigation of Southern Cross, initiated by the South Australian Corporate Affairs Commission and involving the police, was nearing completion, and he had to ensure that the SFE was well distanced from the trader's activities.

The police raided Southern Cross not long afterwards, on 28 October. In the raid, carried out simultaneously on Southern Cross offices in Australia and New Zealand by one hundred police, all books and computer records of the company and associated businesses were seized.

The Australian Financial Review reported on 29 October that Southern Cross Commodities had first attracted the attention of the Australian authorities in December 1980:

> Southern Cross had placed an advertisement in [the December 1980] issue of the US magazine *Commodities*, which outlined six examples of how to make between $US283 and $US383 profit from Sydney–Chicago spreads in 100 ounces of gold. '. . . When you view the world from our perspective . . . you, too, will see the advantages of spreading Sydney and Chicago gold,' the advertisement said. That advertisement was withdrawn from the magazine because of pressure from the Reserve Bank of Australia, whose exchange control regulations prohibit speculative trading on overseas futures markets. Trading offshore by Australian residents is permitted only for genuine hedging and trading operations . . . In a subsequent interview with the *Financial Review* in June 1981, the former

> 'international research director' of Southern Cross, Jack Wesley Savage, made it quite clear that anyone could trade offshore through Southern Cross Commodities. He claimed that futures brokers throughout Australia were doing it without Reserve Bank approval, therefore why shouldn't Southern Cross? Savage left Australia earlier this year [1982], soon after it was revealed that he had been banned from trading on American commodity markets for ten years until December 1990. Documents provided by the US Commodity Futures Trading Commission (CFTC) stated that Savage had indirectly cheated customers in a sophisticated scheme to defraud by engaging in prearranged commodity futures transactions in violation of the Commodity Exchange Act. The day after the article about Savage appeared in the *Financial Review*, Southern Cross Commodities released a statement saying that he had never been an employee of the company. The manager of Southern Cross's Adelaide office [no longer with the group] said that Southern Cross had only used Savage's consultant services and those had been 'discontinued'.

But in January 1982 Southern Cross placed an advertisement proclaiming: 'We back Jack!' and said:

> When Southern Cross began commodity trading, we wanted to be sure we were winners. To do this we needed a highly experienced and skilled team. We hired an excellent team of professional Americans, and in less than a year achieved a business volume greater than the entire trade of the Sydney Futures Exchange.
>
> We brought Harry Schultz to Australia for the most spectacular series of investment seminars held anywhere in the world during 1981. Schultz' advice, Sell Sell Sell, has proved right on.
>
> Customers who took his advice have made large sums. We also engaged, as a consultant, another famous American, Mr Jack Wesley Savage. His success in organising with groups of his wealthy and powerful friends some spectacular 'short squeezes' on American Commodity Exchanges, earned him a ten-year ban from trading in the USA. The regulations under which Mr Savage was banned in the USA by the CFTC do not exist in Australia. In fact, the cattle contract on the Sydney Futures Exchange was short squeezed several times last year (not by Southern Cross) . . .
>
> To join the winning team, fill in this coupon . . .

The *Financial Review* reported that a few months after he left Australia, Savage was revealed in a US Senate report to have been indicted by a US grand jury for allegedly importing 'huge quantities' of marijuana and cocaine into the US. A warrant was issued for his arrest but was returned unexecuted, the paper said. Savage, who had been deported from Canada in 1977, was by October 1982 working in London with Susan Martin, wife of Keith Martin, the chairman of Southern Cross. The *Financial Review* reported on 29 October that it had 'first begun investigating the activities of Southern Cross Commodities in May 1981'. The paper also reported that, around January 1982, after receiving numerous complaints from clients claiming to have lost money through Southern Cross through no fault of their own, the South Australian Corporate Affairs Commission began the investigations which culminated in the massive raid.

The activities of bucket shops were to be an irritation for the SFE in ensuing years, as unregistered brokers over whom the SFE had no jurisdiction cheated their clients of money. It was not until 1986, and the introduction of the Futures Industry Code, that the lid was put on such practices.

5
The cattle squeeze that killed the contract

In May 1982, in an attempt to woo rural producers, especially those in Queensland, the exchange introduced a new contract in export bullocks. To avoid confusion, the name of the live cattle contract was changed to 'trade steer futures'. The following year, as part of the drive to raise the profile of the SFE in the rural community, the SFE appointed a rural liaison officer, Tim Arnott, a graduate with a degree in agricultural economics from the University of New England, with a brief to design and promote the rural contracts. Arnott had won a research prize awarded by the SFE for his paper 'A comparison of the effectiveness of hedging five categories of cattle at delivery and non-delivery selling centres'. Despite the SFE's efforts, the rural contracts were not supported by the farmers. Although futures markets had their genesis in the trade in agricultural commodities, Australian farmers resolutely kept their distance from the SFE's contracts. They were interested in what futures prices told them about market trends but, being traditionally conservative, were reluctant to trade. Some had entered the market, but had tended to gamble, got burned and withdrew, never to return. But there remained widespread demand throughout the 1980s for a daily wool futures quote—even though the contract was not traded and there were no open positions—possibly because it was the only daily price indicator.

August 1982: SFE chairman John Oliver (left) presents a cash prize of $1000 to Tim Arnott, a former student of the University of New England and later a staff member of the SFE, for his research into cattle futures.

The tensions created by the Simonius/Southern Cross episode had barely receded when another problem arose to confront Rutledge and the SFE, this time involving the December 1982 trade steer contract. The circumstances surrounding delivery of that contract became a huge controversy that overhung the SFE and raised serious questions about market practice. While the events and potential problems associated with Simonius were dealt with swiftly, the dispute involving the 'cattle squeeze' was more prolonged and had long-term effects on the market.

It was evident by around 11 or 12 November that a large bought position was being built up in the December trade steer contract and from 15 November the signs of a potential squeeze were clear. Buyers were building positions to a point where they could 'squeeze' the shorts (those who had taken sold positions and who would have to buy to close out or deliver). Such a sudden increase in open interest in a contract running close to expiry is fairly rare, and would arouse curiosity. Moreover, at this time in 1982, prolonged drought had resulted in a decline in the quality of cattle, most of which did not comply with the SFE's delivery standards. If there were insufficient cattle for delivery, the holders of sold contracts (the shorts) could be forced to buy from a group who could dictate prices. Futures prices were already well above those in the drought-affected physical market.

ICCH became concerned about the December contract and on 19 November asked an SFE member, Hill Samuel Australia Ltd, about its intentions and those of its client. ICCH had reacted to a significant increase in Hill Samuel's uncovered bought positions in the December contract which, over a two-week period, had risen from less than 10 per cent of gross open positions to about 57 per cent. The emergence of such a large open position suggested a squeeze could be brought about. Phil Gardiner, then a director of Hill Samuel and deputy chairman of the SFE, said that Hill Samuel's response was that its client intended to take delivery of a large proportion of the bought positions, and as to the suggestion of possibly engineering a squeeze, that its client was in business for profit. However, Gardiner said that Hill Samuel also emphasised that, were a situation to develop which threatened to severely distort the market, it would take regulatory action over its client (which it had the power to do).

By 22 November the December futures prices were rising against the physical trend and on the following day ICCH contacted those holding both long and short positions to determine their intentions regarding delivery. The uncovered open positions were held mostly by clients of two SFE members, Hill Samuel (whose clients accounted for about two-thirds) and Dalgety Futures Pty Ltd (about one-quarter). Unlike the buyers, the sellers were quite diverse and represented by about nine broking firms; the largest holdings were for clients of Jackson Securities Ltd, BHM Futures Pty Ltd and Ord Minnett Securities Pty Ltd. At least 550 of the 653 uncovered contracts were intended to accept delivery, ie, they would buy the physical cattle at one of the SFE's approved delivery centres. This was a further concern because, at the time, the SFE's delivery process could not handle more than 300 contracts within the agreed delivery time.

The buyers continued to increase their open positions and the December futures price continued to rise against the physical market. That, and the impossibility of delivering the number of cattle involved, prompted ICCH to consider trying to cool the market by increasing the deposit on the December contract. It also considered acting under an SFE by-law regarding 'excessive positions capable of affecting the market'. ICCH delayed action but kept in close contact with the buyers' main brokers, both of whom assured ICCH that, since their clients were not intending to damage the market or drive up prices, the situation would not get out of control. The two brokers resumed their buying and the price continued to rise.

ICCH informed Rutledge on 1 December that open December contracts amounted to 1035, of which 653 were uncovered; that is, no offsetting contracts were held by the same broker, so the contracts would probably have to be fulfilled by delivery. Of the 1035, 785 contracts were held by what became known as 'the buying group'. ICCH also announced that, from 2 December, the December contract would be isolated from other delivery months for the purpose of deposits and margins, that there would be no offset of deposits in the spot (December) month and that the deposit would be raised for all participants from $400 to $1000 to ensure that there was adequate cover against market movements or delivery obligations.

Acting under the SFE by-laws, ICCH appointed a special sub-committee to consider the situation. The committee, which included Jim Sinclair, managing director of ICCH, Les Hosking, head of clearing services at ICCH (secretary of the committee), David Rutledge, Gordon Green, Les Pegg and Warwick Poulden of the merchant bank BT Australia Ltd (later Bankers Trust Australia), concluded that an 'excessive' position existed, capable of affecting the market, and that an undesirable situation could develop because it was possible that the Newmarket delivery centre in Melbourne—where most deliveries were to take place—would not be able to cope with the number of cattle involved. The bulk of the deliveries were due in Melbourne because the best available cattle were coming from the Gippsland district rather than drought-affected New South Wales or the Riverina. But it would be impossible to deal with the numbers in one two-week session, even working from dawn until midnight, because the appraisal process was slow, with cattle having to be mouthed, branded and locked up.

The SFE board appointed its own committee to report on the situation. Its findings confirmed those of the ICCH inquiry: there was a concentration of bought positions in what appeared to be very few hands, so that the buyers held considerable power; December futures were at a significant premium over physical prices; the holder of some 700 bought positions had indicated a preference to take as many deliveries as possible although the SFE's delivery system could handle a maximum of only 300 in the 15–30 December delivery period. The exchange ruled on 3 December that delivery would be extended to 17 January—a doubling of the period—and that from Monday 6 December trading in the December contract would be restricted to liquidation of open contracts except for new short selling to give delivery. Such a restriction effectively put the lid on further speculation in the contract. 'The purpose of these decisions is to ensure orderly liquidations of the December positions having regard to the stated intentions of market participants,' the exchange said. Rutledge commented at the time: 'The procedures are usually taken to prevent a concentration of power that could impair the function of the market.' Precedents existed. The delivery period had been extended in August 1981 because of a telecommunications strike, and a liquidation-only rule imposed in September 1981 to counter an attempted squeeze. Rutledge had said on that occasion: 'I have taken the view that the exchange has to be seen to be acting in a responsible way so that genuine users will have confidence in the market.'

The SFE said the extended delivery would enable sufficient cattle to be acquired and give those with sold positions more time. This move did not please those with long positions because, they said, it was biased in favour of the sellers. If indeed the buyers had not intended to acquire cattle, but were engaged in a paper-shuffle for profit, then the SFE's moves destroyed their market play.

The buyers retaliated by taking the SFE to court, trying unsuccessfully to overturn the exchange's decisions to extend the delivery period and impose a 'liquidation-only' order on the December contract. They also challenged an SFE announcement indicating that if 'market congestion' continued it might order contracts to be cash-settled at a price set by the exchange. Rutledge gave evidence in court proceedings that dragged on for several days as the cattle market became bogged down by uncertainty.

On 15 December the SFE board decided to approve Dandenong, near Melbourne, as an emergency alternative delivery centre to supplement Newmarket. Two days later the board announced that all December trade steer contracts still open on 21 December would be cash-settled, with the price to be announced after the close of trading on that day. A sub-committee was established to determine a fair price. John Beaumont, managing director of Anaray Pty Ltd, speaking on behalf of the buyers, called on the SFE to let market forces resolve the controversy and said that a forced cash settlement of the contract would kill the market for speculators. The SFE responded that it would 'take whatever action within its powers which it regarded as necessary to protect the integrity of the overall marketplace'.

The SFE board met on 22 December to hear the views of various floor members, examine written submissions from brokers representing the buyers and the sellers and consider the points raised by some of the buyers. The buyers contended that the exchange's intervention was unfairly founded, hasty and biased in favour of the sellers. They argued that the sellers were speculators who had entered the market late in the contract cycle without much chance of acquiring cattle, knowing the type of market they had got into, and should have been left to wear the consequences of their own actions. Even if the sellers did not know what they were getting into, their brokers—who had been aware of the buying orders from mid-November—should have informed them, said the buyers. According to *The Australian Financial Review*, Anaray's Beaumont described the SFE's cash-settlement decision as 'unfair and a heavy blow to free-market trading'. He said the sellers in the December contract should have been experienced investors who knew what they were doing in such a high-risk market. 'There is no reason why they should be protected or bailed out by the exchange,' he protested. Rutledge said it was 'a complete misinterpretation' to suggest that the exchange seemed to be favouring one side of the market. 'The exchange

The popular myth that cattle with huge horns were driven up O'Connell Street to meet large deliveries.

obviously felt that with the concentration of positions the market was no longer a free market,' he said. 'Our action was not taken lightly.' Extending the delivery period and imposing a liquidation-only order was the 'least intrusive' action the SFE could have taken to deal with what it saw as a serious problem.

For their part, the sellers said that the buyers had deliberately built up a dominant position which they knew to be far in excess of what the SFE's delivery system could handle. The sellers were, overall, less vocal than the buyers, a fact the buyers attributed to the sellers' certainty that the exchange was looking after their interests.

The price was set on 22 December and the contract closed out on 24 December. Delivery involved a record 412 contracts, almost double the previous high of 223 reached only twice before, in June and September 1981. During 1982 deliveries had only twice topped 100. An urban myth persists that cattle with giant horns were driven up Sydney's O'Connell Street, as depicted in newspaper cartoons. It did not happen (besides, deliverable cattle were poll breeds, and had been dehorned).

The SFE had earlier made clear its approach. Speaking at a seminar in August 1981, more than twelve months before the furore over the trade steer contract, Rutledge gave an indication when he said:

> . . . all market participants should be aware of the powers and indeed the responsibilities of the board of the exchange when it perceives that an 'undesirable situation or practice' exists or is about to exist in the market . . . It is nonsense for anyone to claim that the exchange is 'changing the rules' when the board takes action under these or other of the exchange by-laws, such as those dealing with prevention of delivery. The exchange could, on occasions, be just as validly criticised for *not* taking action rather than acting properly under its by-laws . . . I can assure you that the exchange will not stand idly by and see the long-run growth prospects for the futures industry in this country jeopardised by the selfish and narrow-minded actions of only a few market participants.

The December trade steer contract was a source of considerable bad publicity for the SFE and for the trade steer contract. The episode aroused strongly polarised feelings. Those on the buying side were seen to have acted wrongly—and that included the brokers acting for them—in building up such a large position in the December contract. Those on the selling side were also accused of naive or inept behaviour in getting into a sold position in the spot month when it was clearly going to be difficult to deliver. The SFE was criticised by some for being too soft. Others said the SFE should not have become involved. The settlement price the SFE struck was criticised as being a sop to those who had shorted (sold) the market. A key issue was whether any member of the SFE was using its financial strength and that of its client to destabilise the market.

In February 1983 the SFE instituted an investigation into the trade steer debacle by Frank Ryan, a former chairman of the NSW Corporate Affairs Commission and, from early 1982, an independent director of the exchange. Through illness, he had not attended any of the board meetings while matters relating to the December contract were under consideration. Ryan's report was an attempt to defuse the issue. Its findings were those of an objective third party, but one who had the interests of the SFE at heart. Ryan carried out an extensive study, calling in all parties involved. Two initiatives resulted from the investigation: David Rutledge undertook to examine measures for the early detection and monitoring of unduly large open positions; and David Marina, chairman of the SFE's meat and livestock committee, was asked to examine ways of revising the cattle contract and developing a mandatory cash settlement.

The December 1982 cattle squeeze undoubtedly contributed to the SFE's shift away from being an agricultural exchange. It also highlighted weaknesses in the cattle contract, eg, a lack of deliverable cattle in Australia, the fact that the contract was deliverable at centres spread Australia-wide and the inevitable subjectivity involved in appraising individual cattle for delivery. The episode was a turning point in another way: until then, the SFE had relied on ICCH to monitor the futures markets but, if any problems arose, responsibility fell on the SFE. It had become clear that the SFE would have to play a greater role in monitoring market behaviour.

In his address to the 1982 annual general meeting, chairman John Oliver pointed out that it had been a busy year. In addition to its regular monthly meetings, the board had held 50 special meetings and innumerable special committee meetings had been convened. Turnover on the trading floor, however, had been disappointingly low, with volumes in the exchange's main contracts—wool, trade steer and gold—falling by 50 per cent from those seen in 1981. Recession, depressed world metal and commodity markets, and a continuation of Australia's worst drought all contributed to the drop in activity. In contrast, the 90-day bank-accepted bill futures contract was gaining strength, trading daily volumes of more than 1000 contracts, about ten times the 1981 average. Increased uncertainty about the direction of interest rates and currencies also helped boost activity in $US futures with volume rising by 34 per cent. Earlier in 1982 the SFE had broken new ground when it launched options on the $US and 90-day bank bill contracts. They were the first options offered on financial instrument contracts anywhere in the world. The exchange also introduced commission discounts for associate members trading large volumes of contracts. These applied to associate members who fulfilled certain conditions, including being members of the clearing house. Round-turn commissions for non-members trading in gold were also cut, from $70 to $50, in July 1982. Deposits on straddles (the simultaneous purchase of a future in one contract month and the sale of a future in another contract month in the same commodity) were restructured so that ICCH determined the minimum deposit, taking into account the volatility of the individual straddle positions. The move was intended to encourage the use of straddles—an important means of generating overall market liquidity—by setting a straddle deposit, covering two contracts, which was generally considerably less than the deposit required for a single outright position.

An issue that had been troubling the SFE for some time was the question of non-resident participation in its futures markets and its converse, Australian participation in overseas markets. At the time, non-residents could trade the SFE's rural futures contracts, provided they were genuine hedgers. Likewise, genuine Australian hedgers could trade on overseas futures markets. Conscious of looming competition from Hong Kong and Singapore—both of which were planning to launch financial futures markets—the SFE had been lobbying the Reserve Bank and Treasury to relax exchange-control regulations so that non-residents could participate fully in Australian futures markets. In anticipation of the launch of a share-price index futures contract, Rutledge had written to the RBA in November 1982, pointing out that there was 'no exchange-control limitation on purchases of shares by non-residents on the Australian stock exchange'. The SFE requested a similar policy for futures. The RBA replied on 13 January 1983:

> It is considered that, as with applications for non-residents to participate in Australian gold, interest-rate and currency futures markets, examination of such applications should be deferred pending the outcome of the Government's deliberations on the recommendations of the Campbell Committee Report. We therefore advise that the requisite exchange control authorities . . . would not, in the present circumstances, be forthcoming.

Despite the exchange-control regulations, a number of broking firms made extensive use of overseas futures markets and encouraged their clients to do likewise. In a separate letter to Rutledge on 13 January, the RBA said that it had recently written to all companies holding 'general authorities under the Banking (Foreign Exchange) Regulations to deal as principal in commodity futures markets overseas'.

> We brought to their attention the terms of those general authorities and, in particular, the requirement that transactions in overseas futures markets may be undertaken to hedge positions only arising from *bona fide* transactions specified in the authorities.

The letter reminded SFE members using overseas futures markets of the rules under which they could do so. It also reminded the SFE that while it had power over members stepping out of line, it had no authority over other brokers—not members of the exchange—who were offering facilities to trade overseas commodities. For an exchange conscious of the damage done to the futures industry by the Southern Cross episode, this was a cause of considerable concern. The SFE felt it should emphasise to the public that all its members operated under regulations approved by the CAC, with minimum-capital requirements and rules governing the use of clients' funds. As a further protection for clients, the SFE board approved the concept of a fidelity fund but, in view of pending futures industry legislation, delayed its introduction so that the fund could form part of the new legislation.

6
The SPI, the local and other curiosities

Of the contracts developed in the early 1980s, the most successful was the share-price index (SPI) futures contract launched in February 1983. The timing was fortuitous, at the beginning of what was to be a prolonged and worldwide boom in sharemarkets. And the SFE launched the first stock-index futures contract outside the US, only a year after the US had started trading this contract on the Kansas and Chicago markets.

Rutledge recalled that he and Phil Gardiner, then deputy chairman of the exchange and an executive director of Hill Samuel Australia, explained to the NSW Attorney-General, Frank Walker, how the SPI contract would work. Amendments were required to the NSW Futures Market Act because the SPI contract was cash-settled. The share-price index futures contract would use for settlement the All-Ordinaries index, representing a clearly definable market value.

The SPI contract was a hit from the start. Launching the contract on 16 February, the chairman of the Sydney Stock Exchange, Frank Mullens, said he had to admit to feeling 'a touch of envy' that it was the SFE which was able to offer a futures contract in the All-Ordinaries index.

> But having said that I also say how delighted we of the Sydney Stock Exchange are at the creation of yet another market mechanism. I congratulate you on being the first

> exchange outside the US to introduce this financial instrument . . . No doubt due to brilliance of forethought, you have picked an exciting time to launch this contract. Your timing could not have been better. The uncertainty of elections should make all potential users of this market conscious of the benefit this contract offers.

The contract did indeed trade vigorously, accounting for 26.5 per cent of trading volume in its first month and for 36.8 per cent of the SFE's annual volume in 1983.

Two weeks after this auspicious launch, the morale of the markets took a blow when the floor member Ross McConnel Kitchen was suspended from trading on the SFE after breaching exchange regulations requiring members to maintain net tangible assets of at least $100 000. RMK, which had been substantially weakened by the crashing gold price in early 1980, and was rescued from near-annihilation by a debt-for-equity swap by major creditors, was again adversely affected by a plunging gold price which fell from $US504.50 to $US408.50 in a week on the London and New York markets. RMK's membership was subsequently transferred to Gulf South Shipping Company Pty Ltd.

A watershed for the SFE was the federal government's decision in December 1983 to float the $A and remove most exchange controls. The move was a key stage in a process of deregulating and internationalising Australia's financial markets that had been in train since the late 1970s. Rutledge immediately identified opportunities for the SFE to expand into international futures trading. Through his earlier association with Comex he had a close personal relationship with the New York exchange's president and chairman. Within a week of the float of the $A he was discussing with Comex the possibility of a link between the two exchanges' gold contracts that would enable the Comex gold contract to be traded on the SFE floor. Comex, with its dominant role in gold and its position as third-largest futures exchange after the Chicago Mercantile Exchange and the Chicago Board of Trade, had considerable glamour, as Rutledge well knew. And there was the precedent of the Singapore–CME link, with the Singapore exchange SIMEX successfully trading the CME's eurodollar contract. If Singapore could bring a Chicago contract to its exchange, why not bring a New York contract to Sydney? A

SFE chief executive, David Rutledge, (left) on the floor of the exchange in 1984 with former colleague Alan Brody, president of Comex, during Brody's initial visit to Sydney to discuss the proposed link between the two exchanges.

prerequisite, however, was substantial domestic interest in the contract, as well as domestic trading and liquidity. Rutledge travelled to New York in January 1984 to draft an agreement. He was not alone in such negotiations. At the Sydney Stock Exchange, managing director Peter Marshman was working with the Amsterdam Options Exchange to establish a gold link. The SFE, though, stole the glory. After twelve months of negotiations, an agreement between Comex and the SFE was signed early in 1985. The move was seen as a first step in extending trading facilities to meet the growing demand for a 24-hour gold futures market. It was envisaged that Sydney would benefit from the high liquidity of the Comex gold contract, while Comex would secure an extension of its trading hours into a promising new region. It was an exciting move for both exchanges, bringing the SFE into closer contact

Bob White, managing director of Westpac Banking Corporation and chairman of the Australian Banker's Association, launches the two-year Commonwealth government bond contract, 28 February 1984.

with the US regulators and putting the Sydney exchange firmly on the world futures map.

The broadening of international horizons topped what had been a satisfying year for the SFE. Turnover in 1983 had risen by more than 19 per cent, mostly because of the new SPI contract. Gold dropped off sharply, reflecting an absence of volatility in metals prices, and turnover in trade steers remained low. Unlike gold, though, silver traded well, and the 90-day bank-accepted bill and $US futures contracts performed steadily. Wool put on a dismal show, with trade dropping by 28 per cent, largely because of low domestic demand and a correspondingly high level of buying by the Australian Wool Corporation. In an attempt to boost activity in fat lamb futures, floor members voted to amend the specifications of the fat lamb futures contract to make it more attractive to hedgers. The contract size was reduced from 260 to 130 lambs.

The SFE launched a new contract in February 1984 that was to open up another promising dimension, a futures contract based on a notional two-year commonwealth government bond. The contract was launched by R.J. (Bob)

White, then chairman of the Australian Bankers' Association. There was considerable support for this contract, which would offer opportunities for hedgers and speculators in longer-term interest rates. Getting the new contract into place involved discussions with the Reserve Bank and Treasury which, until then, had remained fairly distant from the SFE (in contrast to the NSW CAC, which had a role in approving the exchange's business rules). RBA and Treasury approval was necessary for the introduction of the commonwealth government bond contract. The contract also required amendment of the Futures Market Act to accommodate cash settlement.

The contract was seen as having an infinitely better chance of succeeding if it were cash-settled rather than closed by physical delivery. A model existed: the eurodollar contract traded on the International Monetary Market in Chicago.

The eurodollar contract on the IMM (and on the London futures market) was the first to go to a panel to derive a settlement price. The same practice was used for the SFE bond contract. The Reserve Bank had expressed concern about the prospect of physical delivery of commonwealth bonds, believing that the process left the market vulnerable to a price squeeze which would be bad for the bond market and the efficiency of monetary policy. A second problem regarding physical delivery rested on the fact that commonwealth bonds were 'securities' under the prevailing Securities Industry Act, so a deliverable futures contract would also have been deemed a 'security'. The SFE would have had to take the status of a 'securities exchange' or secure a formal exemption, either of which would have been difficult to obtain at that time because there was no Futures Industry Act. In retrospect, the wisdom of cash settlement on bonds seemed obvious. However, at that time the other SFE cash-settled contracts (currencies and share-price index) were settled against a clearly identifiable cash-market indicator, the Reserve Bank midrate in the case of currencies and the All-Ordinaries in the case of the SPI contract. The notion of a panel of cash-market participants making the settlement price was a novel feature in the Australian context.

The year 1984 was another landmark period for the SFE. In June, as part of the general drive to deregulate financial markets, the SFE abandoned fixed commissions. As had occurred on the stockmarket two months earlier, commissions became negotiable. The pressures of deregulation, specifically negotiable commissions, forced a review of the SFE's membership structure. Under a regime of fixed commissions, associate members were entitled to a 50 per cent discount on commissions payable to a floor member. With commissions negotiable, the regulated 50 per cent discount for associate members became meaningless; rates were negotiable by any trader, associate or not. In a deregulated environment, therefore, there was no incentive to remain an SFE associate member. This was a concern to the exchange for two reasons. First, there were several hundred associate members and their annual membership fees were an important source of SFE revenue. Second, the associate members constituted the largest body of users of SFE markets. To deregulate commission rates and completely obliterate the value of an associate membership would generate significant ill-will for the SFE among this important group.

A further element relevant to the issue of restructuring the membership was the new Futures Industry Act, which was to create self-regulating bodies known as 'futures associations'. The act required anyone dealing with the public to be a member of a futures exchange or association; this was a prerequisite to obtaining a broker's licence, and increased the value of associate membership. The SFE secured verbal agreement from ICCH that no party could become a clearing member unless already a full or associate member. The net tangible asset requirement for floor members was raised to $250 000 from $100 000. And a new class of members, 'locals', was introduced—individuals physically on the trading floor, trading on their own accounts. Local membership was modelled on similar facilities on the major US exchanges. It was designed to attract individuals with entrepreneurial flair and sufficient capital backing to be able to take speculative short-term positions in futures markets, thus enhancing the markets' liquidity. The introduction of locals was a contentious issue. Rutledge, who had raised the idea not long after becoming chief executive, recalled there was widespread opposition to the suggestion from all but a few who wished to take up the proposed new status. Floor members' fears focused on two points: concerns regarding the character, financial standing and behaviour standards of locals for whom a floor member might clear, and a fear that locals might somehow develop client relationships which would take business away from floor members.

In Rutledge's view, having locals accepted was very important for the SFE's international image and role. As others went overseas and saw the contribution made by locals to the US markets, their interest and support grew. Full associate members were able to transfer the value of that membership to local status with no financial cost, provided they could satisfy the floor member through whom they intended to clear that they had sufficient financial backing to trade on the floor. Market associates had the option of parcelling together five market associate memberships and buying a local membership from the SFE. To facilitate consolidation of market associates the SFE helped bring together buyers and sellers of associate membership (although the exchange did not set the prices at which associate memberships changed hands). For a while there was active trading in associate memberships.

The honour of being the first local accepted by the SFE fell to Bill King, until then with Nichols Commodities Pty Ltd and a member of the SFE floor committee. King went on to serve on the locals committee. The second local admitted was David Marina who, with a strong background in the rural industry, was a long-serving chairman of the cattle committee and for many years a board member of the SFE.

The SFE emulated the big Chicago exchanges in one other way—by changing to trading pits. The decisions to introduce locals, and to switch to pits, proved correct. The move to internationalise was also, ultimately, to prove correct, although it was the successful launch of SYCOM (Sydney Computerised Overnight Market) in 1989 that vindicated the thrust, rather than the earlier overseas links.

The SFE in 1984 was also busy revamping its by-laws and restructuring regulations in anticipation of the 1986 Futures Industry Code. In October 1984 the federal government released its draft of a proposed Futures Industry Bill which would bring the industry under the aegis of the national business and finance watchdog, the National Companies and Securities Commission (NCSC). The draft bill sparked widespread discussion among industry participants and others.

The SFE responded with its own views in a lengthy submission to the government. However, the exchange in principle welcomed the move as one that would lift standards in the industry and improve protection for the public—and it would apply a brake for the first time on the activities of non-SFE members. There was still a philosophical division within both the exchange and ICCH about the extent to which the exchange should take responsibility for its members' conduct towards their clients. The clearing house saw itself as having no legal relationship with a member's customer; it tended to regard a futures contract between an exchange member and client as a separate, even unrelated, contract to that entered into by a member on the exchange; so the contract between member and client did not concern the exchange or the clearing house. The issue of client protection was thus not an exchange problem. That was not Rutledge's view. He was impressed by regulations protecting clients' interests in US markets and favoured the introduction of similar structures in Australia. The exchange had already taken a step in 1983 towards lifing the standing of the futures industry with the introduction of registered representatives. It was an important attempt to ensure a minimum level of competency among member firms dealing with the public. 'It was part of a drive to build a level of credibility,' said Rutledge. The move was in line with the US approach and required those dealing with the public to take a test. Many whom the exchange would have preferred to exclude were protected by a 'grandfather' provision. But a new era had begun and subsequently all those dealing with the public had to pass an examination.

An important advance during 1984 was the introduction of a compulsory professional indemnity (PI) scheme. This insurance scheme was seen as a further safety net, in addition to a proposed fidelity fund, for clients of the SFE. The scheme covered civil liability incurred by brokers, with very few exceptions—not an easy coverage to secure from underwriters. The objective was to provide an umbrella policy under which the SFE was the insured party on behalf of all members dealing with the public. The SFE was to collect premiums from members—a specified basic sum from floor members and a lesser amount from associates, plus an additional amount related to each member's level of business. If a broker made a mistake and lost money, there would be no risk of a client suffering financially. PI took some time to finalise during 1984 but was introduced before the fidelity fund and well ahead of the Futures Industry Bill.

The SFE followed its introduction of a two-year government bond contract with a similar contract based on ten-year government bonds. Launched in December 1984 by Ken Booth, then NSW Treasurer, the contract traded well from the start. Two other contracts launched in 1984 which did not live up to expectations and were suspended because of a lack of liquidity were a contract based on the All-Industrials index and one based on the Minerals and Metals index.

Financial futures activity increased encouragingly during 1984, particularly in the case of the SPI, 90-day bank-accepted bill and $US futures. The star performer was the SPI contract, which turned in a record performance of 237 011 contracts, up 32 per cent on 1983. Volumes in $US futures rose 40 per cent, following the increased volatility in foreign-exchange markets. The bank-accepted bill futures contract, while showing only a modest 7 per cent increase, nevertheless had its best year to date. The robust trading in financial futures offset the downturn in gold, silver, wool and trade steers. By the end of 1984 plans for the introduction of exchange-traded options, instruments that would later provide an enormous boost to SFE activity, were almost complete.

While 1984 had seen a number of important achievements, the period was not all plain sailing for the exchange's executives and staff. As the profile of the SFE rose, so apparently did its propensity to attract trouble—or unwelcome attention. One clash between the exchange and an associate member company, Kingston Commodities Pty Ltd, over the company's failure to comply with accounting and other requirements, resulted in a series of court actions in which both sides suffered defeats. In the end, the exchange emerged at least technically victorious in that Kingston resigned its membership, but at one stage of the skirmish the exchange was found by a Supreme Court judge to have failed to follow the correct procedures of natural justice in its internal disciplinary process. The procedures were subsequently overhauled to ensure that dispute proceedings would always follow the rules of natural justice. The incident emphasised to the exchange the importance of developing skilled in-house legal resources.

The exchange also found itself virtually besieged—for reasons which never became quite clear—by an eccentric individual who, denied associate membership, bombarded Rutledge with lengthy, rambling letters. Unable to stem the barrage, the wearied chief executive could only pass them on to the SFE's lawyers, Laurence & Laurence, with a request to 'please reply'. Following this inconclusive correspondence, the man, who was often seen moving about the city on roller skates with a transistor radio plugged into his ear, took to appearing regularly at the offices of Laurence & Laurence, where he would give vent to a tirade against the SFE and Rutledge. Earlier, the protester had been responsible for a rapid upgrading of the exchange's security arrangements following an incident in which he became enraged at a delay in the reading room, stormed into the office of publicity and education manager Stephen Calder and threatened to put the slightly built Calder's head through the window.

The futures exchange was not the man's only target. For months in 1983 he had disrupted lectures at the Securities Institute of Australia, a campaign of harassment which ended only when the institute obtained a Supreme Court injuction to restrain him. Eventually he ended his life in a fall from the Sydney Harbour Bridge.

Bizarre episodes punctuated 1984. In July, the SFE became aware of an intruder in the market when the Mini-Futures Exchange of Australia Ltd placed an advertisement in *The Australian Financial Review* announcing its intention to open for business. An SFE staff member visited the company's offices at 20 Bond Street and established that the embryonic exchange planned to operate in the $US, gold, silver and share-price index futures markets. It had adopted the SFE's rules and contracts and, dividing each contract by four, planned mini-contracts requiring mini-deposits and mini-margins. The venture grew out of a view that the 'tick' movement in the SFE's share-price index futures contract—the smallest possible movement in the market price—was still large enough to deter small-time traders. The mini-exchange planned to attract these customers. However, the proposed exchange, not being an authorised futures exchange, was in breach of the Trade Practices Act. The SFE secured an injunction from the Federal Court preventing the Mini-Futures Exchange and its principal, Ben Garcia, from operating, and was awarded costs—which were never paid.

The curtain had barely been drawn on this episode when another SFE associate member went to the wall. The Glauber Group, operated by an urbane Swiss, Marcel Fachler, collapsed early in August following what he described (in a notice pinned to the door of the group's Sydney office) as 'adverse trading . . . resulting in the depletion of all the companies' capital and reserves'. The SFE was advised on 8 August that Glauber Futures Pty Ltd, a full associate member, had ceased trading. Inquiries into the activities of the Glauber Group revealed that more than $17 million in assets could not be accounted for. The interim receiver was quoted in *The Australian Financial Review*, 17 September: 'It would appear that significant sums of money have travelled overseas.' However no losses were incurred by clients of the SFE associate member, Glauber Futures Pty Ltd.

It was a source of intense irritation to the exchange that its image suffered whenever a small trader lost money, even when the losses were sustained through a non-member operating on the 'fringe'. One loser was particularly vocal and visible. Clad in black theatrical clothes studded with symbols of the occult and topped by a wizard's hat, he daily patrolled the Sydney CBD streets for several months during 1984, pushing a baby's pram loaded with silver trinkets and shouting abuse about the SFE. He had lost money through trading on overseas futures markets and, although the SFE had played no role, he was taking out his rage and disappointment on the exchange. He was a victim of Central Commodities, not a member of the SFE, a broking house at one stage controlled by the family of the high-flying commodities broker Robert Howes and which flouted Reserve Bank regulations by specialising in overseas trading. The black-clad figure would often park his pram beneath Rutledge's office in O'Connell Street. The exchange chief could clearly hear the shouts and insults. On one occasion, in exasperation, Rutledge rang John Currie at Laurence & Laurence. 'He's outside my window—put an injunction on him,' the infuriated Rutledge demanded. That was not possible—perhaps fortunately, for it would have seemed a heavy-handed action by the exchange. Ranald Stewart, the exchange's general manager, finance and administration, exercising what he said was 'enormous restraint', invited the protester—without pram and theatrical clothes—into his office, where Stewart heard a rational account of what had happened. The man, who was in his early thirties, had lost what was to him a considerable fortune, including his own house and his mother's. He saw no difference between the trading on the SFE and the unregulated activities of hustlers like Howes. And the SFE was an easy target; Central Commodities was far more elusive (matters relating to that company were still the subject of legal proceedings at the end of 1992). The vengeful loser continued his daily harangue, his pointed hat and silver trinkets demonstrating to passers-by that he equated futures trading with black magic. In the end, the man was restrained under an obscure Sydney City Council regulation which designated his behaviour an obstruction to pedestrian traffic, and his persecution of the exchange ceased.

David Rutledge's decision to leave the SFE towards the end of 1984 came as a shock to the exchange. He had presided over years of enormous change, meeting huge challenges and upheavals, and defusing some potentially damaging episodes. It had been an immense task, often exhilarating, often exhausting. He had succeeded in building good relationships with government and the regulatory authorities—a dimension further strengthened by the range of contacts of Frank Ryan and John Oliver—and the SFE was now regarded as a stable and reputable institution. Much of what was achieved was a product of his deft persuasion of members and board alike, each of whom had individual vested interests. Rutledge was supported in these efforts by a committed group that included board and committee members such as Ray Arthur, Colin Bell, John Broinowski, Mike Crivelli, Phil Gardiner, Bruce Hudson, David Marina and Paul McNab. And Rutledge persevered with a vision of the SFE's future direction that laid a sound footing for his successor. By 1984, the exchange included in its list of members some financial heavyweights, big institutions which had joined to trade the currency and interest-rate futures and SPI contracts. Rutledge left in December 1984, only a few months before the boom in financial markets began.

Rutledge bequeathed a considerable legacy to the institution he had steered through four-and-a-half turbulent years: it had an improved regulatory structure, an extended range of contracts and an increasingly international focus. He also influenced the exchange's future through encouraging the man who would become his successor to apply for the post. Rutledge had travelled to Switzerland late in 1984 and stopped during the return journey in Kuala Lumpur, where Les Hosking was the Asian regional representative of ICCH. Rutledge told Hosking that he did not intend to stay on at the SFE and that if interested Hosking should apply for the post of chief executive. The position was subsequently advertised and Hosking sent in an application. He was short-listed and invited to Sydney for an interview. Hosking took an overnight flight from Kuala Lumpur to attend a 10am Monday interview, returning on a lunchtime flight that got him back to his office in Kuala Lumpur that night.

From 1980 to 1983 Hosking had been ICCH's clearing services divisional manager, responsible for SFE clearing. He had joined ICCH in 1979 as administration manager in the Sydney branch. Before ICCH, he had been manager of the futures division of C. Itoh & Co (Australia) Ltd, having begun his career in futures as a floor trader. Born in Darlinghurst Road in Sydney's King's Cross, the son of a professional bicycle rider, Hosking lived in the area until he was thirteen—a factor of his early life that, he said, gave him his instincts to 'kill or be killed'. After leaving school he attended the Royal Australian Naval College and became a midshipman at the Jervis Bay naval base. The navy, according to Hosking, refined him into a gentleman, but the life was not for him. After a series of odd jobs, such as swimming pool lifeguard and beach inspector, he joined J.W. McGregor in 1967 and secured his trader's pass the following year.

Hosking was appointed chief executive of the SFE in November 1984 and took up his new position on 2 January 1985. Rutledge and Hosking, both of whom played vital roles in steering the SFE through the turbulent and dynamic 1980s, presented contrasting styles. Rutledge, with an academic background and training, was seen by the floor traders (themselves seen as brash and rumbustious) as somewhat aloof and intellectual. But he had a good sense of the organic functioning of the exchange and succeeded in combining the skills of a politician with those of a manager. He treated staff well, ran a happy ship and provided a degree of autonomy. Les Hosking, with a background as a wool floor trader and then manager at ICCH, developed a more hands-on style. He won a reputation as someone with a short fuse but with the grace to admit mistakes, and as an effective administrator. Hosking was to preside over the SFE's years of explosive growth and to guide the exchange's transition to a sophisticated and highly computerised operation.

Rutledge's association with the SFE was not over. He returned in 1986 as a consultant and independent director, and was a board member and deputy chairman during that year, with a continuing close involvement in the negotiations to establish links with Comex and the London International Financial Futures Exchange (LIFFE, now London International Financial Futures and Options Exchange).

7
From bodyguards to Grosvenor Street

When Les Hosking took the helm at the Sydney Futures Exchange on 2 January 1985, he had more than a rough idea of what he wanted to get done. 'I had a concrete plan,' he says. 'And the board had indicated its own objectives.' Hosking's immediate strategy focused on the exchange's public image, relationship with the press and overall costs and fee structure. Relationships with government were already sound, a result of the efforts of Hosking's predecessor, David Rutledge. The new chief executive was keen to increase turnover on the exchange and saw excessive costs as a deterrent to trading. Much of the $5.50 round-turn fee shared equally by the buyer and seller in each futures transaction went to the International Commodities Clearing House (ICCH) for its clearing and registering services. Hosking had determined from the start that the SFE should handle its own clearing.

Hosking knew that his plans would entail some difficult negotiations and decisions, and his years with ICCH had toughened him for the challenge. ICCH's decision to send him to manage its Kuala Lumpur office had landed him at the centre of a commodity squeeze with elements of high adventure. The squeeze was engineered by a powerful businessman who believed a cartel of palm-oil producers was setting an extortionately high price. He retaliated with heavy selling of futures, trying to drive down the price and break the cartel.

The hectic trading destabilised the market. ICCH, which was funding 30 per cent of the exchange's guarantee, asked Hosking to step in to safeguard its interests. Hosking initiated a doubling of the deposits on the palm-oil contracts. Two hours later two thugs broke down the door to his office and the indignant businessman appeared, demanding that Hosking rescind the increase. When Hosking refused and threatened to call the police, he was told: 'Call the police? I *own* the police!' Hosking got the deposits he wanted, but in the following weeks found himself the target of a barrage of intimidation. The exchange was picketed. Hosking received anonymous sympathy cards commiserating over 'a death in the family'. He was followed and his driver became adept at weaving through carparks to shake off the tail. On the evening of a meeting at which the exchange was to decide how to deal with the palm-oil squeeze, a bullet shattered the rear window of Hosking's car. By this time he had four private bodyguards at his house and another four at his office. The squeeze continued but when outstanding margin calls reached $25 million the clearing house told Hosking to crack down hard. He acted swiftly, setting a price and closing out the palm-oil contracts off-market. He made enemies but he brought order back to the market. And he survived.

Soon after this episode, Hosking left Kuala Lumpur with few regrets and moved to Singapore, where he was assigned to try to win business for ICCH from the new Singapore futures exchange. Hosking's next appointment was to be that of managing director of ICCH's Hong Kong office, a post he was to take up at the end of 1984. But fate intervened. When Hosking got the SFE job, he rang his mother in Sydney to say he would be returning. She was less than wholly impressed: 'Can't you get a better job than that?' was her rebuke. 'These people are always getting bad press.'

Self-clearing, while on Hosking's agenda from the outset, was to take several years to achieve. Meanwhile, in 1985, the SFE set about encouraging additional locals to trade on its floor. The exchange took a full-page advertisement in *The Australian Financial Review*, showing a figure on a single-wheel bicycle juggling, with a caption: 'If you can do this with financial affairs—be a local.' The existing local members were far from pleased by the implications of the advertisement.

The agreement to link gold trading between the SFE and Comex is signed at Boca Raton, Florida, 7 March 1985, by (left to right) Alan Brody, president of Comex; Oscar Burchard, chairman of Comex; John Oliver, SFE chairman; and Les Hosking, chief executive of the SFE.

And they were even less impressed with the SFE's plan to facilitate special work permits to enable US locals to move to Australia and trade on the Sydney exchange's floor. But the plan went ahead because the view prevailed that the market needed the additional liquidity that experienced traders could bring.

A number of important changes were already under way when Hosking became chief executive, including the introduction of exchange-traded options, the proposed link with Comex (New York Commodity Exchange) and the drafting of a Futures Industry Bill. Within a month of Hosking's arrival exchange-traded options were introduced; these instruments were to play an increasing role during the 1980s as traders came to realise their risk-management potential. The Comex link, for which agreement was signed on 7 March 1985 at the Futures Industry Association conference at Boca Raton, Florida, was seen as a significant step in the process of globalising futures markets and in a way that put the SFE at the forefront of the trend. Not all of the increasing activity was welcome: the exchange had on its plate a number of legal problems,

A proud and happy founding chairman, Clive Hall, on the occasion of the SFE's 25th anniversary, 11 May 1985.

largely concerning questionable dealings with clients by a small number of members. These issues, and the need to contribute to the drafting of the Futures Industry Bill, were costly in terms of time and legal fees. Hosking decided that the SFE should hire an in-house lawyer. Tony Dreise, a solicitor who had been working with the NSW Corporate Affairs Commission, answered the advertisement and took up his new post with the SFE in mid-1985.

Hosking was anxious to increase turnover, expand the range of contracts and improve the exchange's public image. The board was keen to attract more institutional activity but the institutions were cautious about the exchange. The SFE

Past and present chairmen: (left to right) John Oliver, Desmond Brook, Clive Hall and Rex Brown.

was still tainted, in the eyes of the public, by the excesses of the gold years and the problems associated with the cattle squeeze in 1982. It was widely seen as a retail, speculative market afflicted by crises and improper practices. 'I always had absolute optimism that we would increase our turnover because of financial deregulation and internationalisation of the financial markets,' said Hosking. Initial efforts to boost turnover were successful. He had told the staff he would stand drinks all round when turnover hit 5000 contracts a day; within six months he was happy to find he had to honour that promise.

In May 1985 the SFE celebrated its 25th anniversary. In the following year the SFE held its first black-tie dinner since Clive Hall's retirement in January 1982, this time to honour another long-serving board member who was retiring, Desmond Brook. Addressing the gathering, chairman John Oliver described Brook as one of the exchange's 'goal-setters—not for just a few years as other board members have—but for 21 of the SFE's 25 years'. During that time Brook had served as

Desmond Brook (left), long-serving board member and former SFE chairman, with John Oliver at a testimonial dinner held in Brook's honour in June 1986.

chairman and deputy chairman for varying periods and had been convenor of many SFE committees. Oliver referred to Hall's retirement, when the then chairman Phil Gardiner had drawn on George Bernard Shaw's praise for the contributions to progress of 'unreasonable' men. 'I put Desmond in the category of being more of a reasonable man,' Oliver said. 'In fact, as a board member, he is one of the most reasonable men I have met.'

In April 1986 the SFE introduced new wool and live cattle contracts, both cash-settled, to replace the greasy wool and trade steer contracts. Removing the obligation to deliver would, it was hoped, broaden the specifications of the contract and thus the range of users. Soon after launching the new contracts the SFE significantly reduced clearing and exchange fees for most futures transactions. Announcing the change, Hosking said that reducing the fees from 1 August would bring the SFE's transaction costs 'closer into line with those on international futures exchanges of similar size'. The new

Brian Williamson, chairman of LIFFE (centre), rings the bell to open business on the SFE on 23 October 1986 and mark the start of the SFE–LIFFE link. Williamson is flanked by the SFE's chairman John Oliver (left), and chief executive Les Hosking.

scheme eliminated concessions applying to 'day trades' (contracts bought and sold on the same day) and 'scratch trades' (day trades bought and sold at the same price), but it represented a 72 per cent reduction in clearing and exchange fees on other trades. The new fee of $2.50 a round turn ($1.25 to buy and $1.25 to sell) compared with a previous charge of $5.50 a round turn and included a levy of 10 cents a trade (20 cents a round turn) for the fidelity fund required under the Futures Industry Code. Hosking said that the SFE was committed to ensuring that transaction costs were attractive and competitive for Australian and international users. 'The main target of the exchange's campaign has been ICCH's fee, which did not compare favourably with clearing charges elsewhere,' Hosking said.

The long-awaited Comex link became a reality in November 1986. A month before, however, on 23 October, the SFE launched a similar arrangement—the first of its kind—with

Dr Susan Phillips, chairman of the US's Commodity Futures Trading Commission, at the launch of the SFE–Comex link, with Irving Redel, chairman of Comex and four members of the Comex board of governors.

LIFFE, which enabled trading in US treasury bonds and eurodollar interest-rate futures, two of the most actively traded futures contracts in the world. Under the link, a position opened on the SFE could be closed on LIFFE and *vice versa*. Trading was launched with the chairman of LIFFE, Brian Williamson, ringing the bell to open business in the Sydney exchange at 8am Sydney time. LIFFE's chief executive officer, Michael Jenkins, was also present. The ceremony was the culmination of some eighteen months of discussions between the two exchanges and heralded a seventeen-hour trading day which was expected to bring enormous gains in activity. At a dinner to celebrate the SFE–LIFFE link, SFE chairman John Oliver said: 'In these fast-moving days business cannot afford to sleep and, put simply, the aim of this historic link is to provide the wide-awake enterprises of the world with a liquid and effective venue for risk-management at a time when other zones are in repose.'

A similar celebration was held on 20 November to mark the start of the link with Comex, the world's largest metals futures market and most liquid gold market. Under this arrangement—a first for both Comex and the SFE—the 100 troy ounce gold futures contracts could be opened or settled on either exchange. The Comex link was launched by Dr Susan Phillips, chairman of the US's Commodity Futures Trading Commission, and was attended by Comex's chairman, Irving Redel, and president, Alan Brody.

The enthusiasm and painstaking preparation that had gone into the arrangements brought eventual disappointment. Neither link was successful. The SFE had correctly identified the tendency towards globalisation of exchanges but, in Hosking's words: 'We just did not have the mechanism to enable the liquidity of Comex to be transferred overnight, and the same applied to the LIFFE contracts.' Although the experiments failed, they helped to raise international awareness of the SFE at a time when it had grown to become the tenth-largest futures exchange in the world. And this growth occurred between 1982 and 1986, years when new exchanges were emerging; LIFFE opened in 1982 and Simex in 1984.

By the end of 1986 the SFE's international reputation was established. The domestic record of strong growth boosted its credibility and enthusiastic ambassadors such as Hosking, Rutledge and Oliver never missed an opportunity when travelling abroad to spread the word about the SFE's potential. Trading on the SFE during 1986 reached new record highs with 3.4 million contracts turned over, an increase of 172 per cent over the previous year. The performance overshadowed the 140 per cent rise in trading recorded in 1985. The surge in activity was attributed to an increased need to protect against fluctuating interest rates, which resulted in a greater awareness of futures and the entry of new players to the markets. The biggest contribution to activity came from the ten-year commonwealth bonds, which increased almost five-fold to 1.4 million lots. The 90-day bank-accepted bill futures were next most active, trading 1 million contracts, an increase of 80 per cent over 1985. Volumes in the All-Ordinaries index futures rose by 65 per cent. The All-Ordinaries and the ten-year bond ranked among the ten most actively traded futures contracts in the world. Exchange-traded options also added to activity. By contrast, the $US, wool and live cattle contracts declined in volume. The significant expansion in trading was reflected in higher earnings for the SFE; the exchange ended the year with an operating surplus of $2.6 million, up from the previous year's $1.16 million. This was achieved despite considerable investment in the two international links and the continuing development of the exchange.

Other landmarks for the futures industry in 1986 were the introduction of the Futures Industry Code, providing a sounder regulatory framework for futures trading in Australia, the appointment of an arbitration panel with formal procedures and the establishment of a fidelity fund maintained by a levy on trades.

It was not long before the new fidelity fund was called on to prove its role as a safety net for investors. In 1986 the Corporate Affairs Commission had begun investigating the Shintoh Group, South-East Asian futures brokers, and in the following year the company, an associate member of the SFE since March 1981, was suspended by the SFE board pending a court hearing. In making a receivership order against Shintoh Pty Ltd and G.H. Shintoh Australia Ltd in October 1987, Justice Nathan in the Victorian Supreme Court said that the CAC alleged that Shintoh 'set up an elaborate scheme clothed with documentation to give purported legality but whose purpose was to beguile Australians out of their money'. The Shintoh group, headed by Richard Lau—who subsequently disappeared overseas—operated for about six years from February 1981 until its funds were frozen in April 1987 by the Supreme Court. The SFE had by then received a number of complaints from clients of the Shintoh Group, whose companies included Golden Harvest and Asiavest and whose activities were portrayed as trading on Japanese commodity markets in exotic commodities such as Tokyo red beans, Maebashi dry cocoons, Yokohama silk and Tokyo raw sugar and rubber. Asiavest, which lost more than $2 million of Queenslanders' funds, had been placed in receivership in January 1987 and the company ceased operating with its assets sold to repay debts and clients. The Victorian crown prosecutor, Bernard Bongiorno QC, was later to say that the companies did not trade but just 'relieved investors of money'. The SFE liaised with the NCSC over the matters relating to Shintoh, although the company had carried out most of its business in purported overseas trading, through a member of the group which did not have SFE membership, and traded minimally on the Sydney exchange. Until forced by the Futures Industry Code to bring its overseas trading under SFE jurisdiction, the company used its SFE membership only for SFE trading. After a trial lasting three months, two principals of Shintoh were found guilty of defrauding Victorian investors of $6.4 million and sentenced to eight years' imprisonment. The SFE fined G.H. Shintoh $250 000 and expelled the company from the exchange, citing innumerable breaches of the exchange's articles as well as several breaches of the Futures Industry Code. The exchange's fidelity fund paid out $176 641 to various claimants following their financial loss from fraudulent misuse of funds by Shintoh. This episode, and the case of another bucket shop, Nizal Investments Pty Ltd—also an associate member of the SFE—where $650 801 was paid out, were the only two occasions when the SFE had to make use of the fidelity fund to reimburse clients for fraud. The two were a lingering reminder of the problems that arose before the Futures Industry Code was in place. Hosking pointed out that the new futures industry law increased the power of the authorities to investigate dealers.

Still, he felt it was necessary to warn Australian investors about the bucket shops. He told investors to be cautious about claims of fantastic gains to be made from futures trading on some Asian exchanges. In the SFE's annual report for 1987, Hosking referred to 'the efforts of state and federal regulators during the early part of the year in eliminating from within Australia certain improper futures trading operations purportedly trading on Asian markets' as a highlight of the year:

> . . . one of the major impacts of the new Futures Industry Code which came fully into force in early 1987 was to require all individuals, firms or corporations conducting futures trading on behalf of Australian residents, whether on the SFE or any other futures exchange, to obtain a licence. A prerequisite for the licence was the mandatory membership of an Australian futures exchange or futures association. These requirements enabled the Exchange and the State and Federal regulators, for the first time, to vet existing and new futures broking operations which had previously been outside each regulatory body's jurisdiction. The result was the disciplining or prosecution, or in many cases voluntary closure, of a number of futures and leveraged currency operators within a very short period of six months. The timely and effective

manner in which the Exchange took action and the clear demonstration of co-operative co-regulation between the Exchange and its regulators has substantially enhanced the reputation of the futures industry in Australia in the eyes of the media, who monitored the events very closely, and in the eyes of the investing public here and abroad.

During 1987 the SFE received a number of suggestions that the ten-year commonwealth bond contract should be deliverable instead of cash-settled. Two main reasons were cited: first, the change would expand trading because strategies such as cash-and-carry and other forms of arbitrage could be more confidently executed; and there was considerable dissatisfaction with the prevailing method of determining the cash-settlement price, largely because it was difficult to get an accurate reflection of the yield of a notional 12 per cent coupon bond. The SFE formed a sub-committee in June 1987 and, after two meetings, the committee decided to survey users of the bond-futures market to test the appeal of amended settlement procedures and the merits of physical delivery. Other questions put to the market related to pricing, length of delivery period and composition of deliverable stock. Responses were equally divided for and against physical delivery, highlighting the complexities involved and leaving the sub-committee with more work to do on the issue. Ultimately, a decision was deferred, but the board kept the possibility of physical delivery under review. Meanwhile, the exchange was also considering the question of whether an additional, shorter-term bond futures contract would be a successful innovation.

Hosking was continuing his drive to boost activity, particularly in the languishing international links, by encouraging more locals on to the Sydney trading floor. He had commented in his 1986 annual report:

Of the highest importance is the expansion and development of a group of committed, active and experienced 'locals'. The Exchange will continue to promote its Local Membership category to resident and non-resident individuals. The urgent necessity however to inject experienced Locals into the Sydney Futures Exchange's international contracts will be of particular emphasis. Non-residents of Australia will be encouraged to purchase or lease Local Memberships and a temporary Local Membership category is available in special circumstances. For all Local Members, incentives are already available in the form of fee rebates for high-volume trading.

In August 1987 the exchange launched its Locals Permit Plan as an inducement to experienced overseas individual traders. It had official approval to sponsor up to 60 non-resident locals to come to Australia and trade on the SFE, with work permits granted by the Department of Immigration. A glossy promotional brochure coaxed the reader to 'trade in liquid contracts on a fast-growing exchange . . . earn valuable fee rebates for trading high volumes . . . escape the Chicago, New York or London winter . . . enjoy Sydney's envied climate and lifestyle'. By cutting red tape and offering incentives—including leased membership for $200 a month, about half the normal cost—the exchange hoped to attract traders whose contribution would lift liquidity. The message was: the SFE was looking for performers.

The growing maturity of the exchange was underscored by the strength with which it weathered the October 1987 worldwide stockmarket crash—Bloody Monday in the US and Black Tuesday in Australia—when the world's stockmarkets plunged into crisis. In the US, the Dow-Jones tumbled 22.62 per cent between the close of trading on Friday 16 October and the end of trading on the following Monday. In Australia, the sharemarket barometer, the All-Ordinaries index, shed 24.3 per cent on Tuesday 20 October, one of the market's largest one-day falls. The financial system came under severe strain, with pressures on credit, clearing and settling transactions. Traders who had come into the financial markets during the previous five years had never seen a bear market and were operating in uncharted waters. While the economic implications of the crash were overestimated, the financial markets and investors suffered badly. However, no member of the SFE defaulted in its commitment to the clearing house, despite very substantial cash calls made at short notice and a number of subsequent failures by customers to pay calls to members. The SFE stayed open throughout the crash and coped with the highest turnover in its history.

Arguments about what fuelled the crash continued for some time; much of the blame was laid at the door of stock-index arbitraging, also known as program trading, with its sharpest critics calling for the practice to be banned. Index futures had been introduced in 1982 and became extremely popular, helping to feed the bull run in sharemarkets because they made it possible to hedge quickly and cheaply. Their growing popularity led the legendary US investor, Warren Buffett, chairman of Berkshire Hathaway Inc, to warn against the burgeoning new concept of stock-index futures; he told the US Congress in 1982 that they were 'likely to be overwhelmingly detrimental to the security-buying public and therefore in the long run to capital markets generally'. The supporters of stock-index futures and options pointed out that they enabled many traders to hedge against losses on their holdings without selling stocks. But the search for the villain that caused the crash was in full swing and, to many, program trading of stock-index futures was the natural target. Many blamed Black Monday on futures markets generally, ignoring the fact that a big benefit of futures is that they provide a hedge to reduce risk. Hosking said at the time: 'Futures, of course, are the ideal scapegoat—a victim for the lynch mob, someone to blame, surrounded in mystery and misunderstanding, an ideal target for a good burning at the stake.' Hosking argued that futures acted as a pressure valve in crises such as that of October 1987; the crash would have been much worse had futures not existed. 'Claims that futures trading, in particular program trading, were the cause of the crash simply cannot be supported by facts,' he said.

The SFE traded 5.37 million futures and options contracts in 1987, a rise of 60 per cent over 1986, giving the exchange its fifth consecutive record year. The biggest growth was in 90-day bank-accepted bill futures, where volume jumped 94 per cent to 2.1 million contracts. The ten-year commonwealth bond contract rose by 36 per cent to 2.06 million contracts. Options trading more than doubled, with the largest increase in All-Ordinaries index options which rose by more than 400 per cent. However, activity in the international links remained lacklustre; likewise, the new cash-settlement procedures for wool and live cattle had not breathed new life into these contracts, as had been hoped. The exchange had made progress elsewhere, in development programs designed to strengthen its reputation and improve the market's liquidity and depth. New price-reporting, trade-matching and surveillance facilities had been introduced. Further plans included a new trading floor and an extension of trading hours through links with other exchanges or screen trading.

In March 1988 the SFE launched an $A contract. The Australian currency had been extremely volatile and $A futures and options were already trading on the Chicago Mercantile Exchange and Philadelphia Stock Exchange. Activity in the new contract was sufficient to prompt the introduction of options as well. Options were already drawing enthusiastic trading; by April 1988 interest-rate options were a star performer, with trading at almost six times the levels of a year earlier.

Les Hosking was increasingly determined to introduce extended trading hours. He was quoted in the *Journal of Commerce* on 14 March 1988: 'We can't treat ourselves as though we're 12 000 miles from the rest of the world. We need 24-hour markets to protect ourselves from US news.' Speaking at a futures industry conference in Boca Raton, Florida, Hosking cited the events of 20 October 1987 when the All-Ordinaries stock-index contract opened 700 points down in reaction to the previous day's crash in the US. 'When we woke up on 20 October we were greeted by the news of a 500-point fall on the New York Stock Exchange. We immediately realised that closing our exchange at night is dangerous,' Hosking said.

Another new contract hit the boards on 17 May 1988 when three-year commonwealth bond futures were launched. They were an immediate success, trading more than 3000 contracts a day. Options on the three-year bond futures were introduced a month later. The month of May notched up more than one million contracts in futures and options, an increase of 124 per cent over May 1987. (It was only three years earlier, in 1985, that *annual* turnover had for the first time exceeded one million contracts.) The 90-day bank-accepted bill futures was the chief contributor, trading 771 601 contracts, but the fastest-growing market was the options on the ten-year commonwealth bonds, where trading levels were three times those of May 1987. The vigorous trading trend was confirmed when figures for the half-year to June showed a 54 per cent increase over the previous corresponding period.

By this stage in 1988 Hosking's three-year plan was com-

Top: *The SFE enjoys lively trading on the floor at 13–15 O'Connell Street during its first evening trading session held to coincide with the Treasurer's economic statement on 25 May 1988.* Below: *Traders take the opportunity during hectic trading on the first evening session on 25 May 1988 to practise sign language in preparation for the move to the new exchange in Grosvenor Street.*

plete and the exchange embarked on a new five-year strategy that would include a move to new premises, complete computerisation, an examination of screen-dealing as an adjunct to the open-outcry trading floor and further steps to enhance its position as a self-contained and self-regulated entity. Business was so profitable that the SFE had been able to accumulate financial reserves to pay for expansion.

While more than half of the demand for SFE contracts was coming from Australian financial institutions, there was increasing interest from overseas, especially the US and UK, where governments had recognised the SFE to be soundly regulated and suitable for trading by their residents. In November 1988 the exchange was able to contemplate an increase in US trading in its contracts, following a watershed US decision allowing non-US members of the SFE to advertise their products to the US public without the need for Commodity Futures Trading Commission (CFTC) registration. This recognition was helped by the fact that Australia's regulatory code was comparable to that of the US. The exchange was granted similar acknowledgment in the UK. This was a further encouragement for the SFE in its planning for extended trading hours. During 1988, the exchange twice opened for a single evening session, one to coincide with the Treasurer's economic statement in May and a second when the federal budget was announced in August. Both occasions had generated big trading volumes.

The SFE reported an increase in pre-tax surplus of 35 per cent to $A4.48 million for the year to December 1988. This was achieved on annual turnover of 7.87 million futures and options contracts and a 41 per cent lift in activity which included the milestone of one million option contracts traded during the year.

The SFE moved into its fifth home in February 1989 when it leased premises in Grosvenor Street in the heart of Sydney's business district. The new trading floor was opened on 3 February by the NSW Premier, Nick Greiner. For traders, the move was none too soon; working conditions at the old floor had become almost intolerable, with the din of demolition in the adjacent building adding to the usual racket of the trading floor. Vibrations from construction work sent wall tiles tum-

Traders gather during the last week of trading at 13–15 O'Connell Street, the SFE's home from July 1979 to February 1989.

bling into trading booths and on one occasion the trading floor had to be evacuated because of a leak of petrol fumes. There were other frustrations when industrial problems delayed the move to the far grander premises in Grosvenor Street. The nineteenth-century historic buildings, Royal Naval House and Federation Hall, were gutted and renovated (but their facades maintained) at a cost of $20 million to the leaseholder, Grosvenor Place. The SFE spent $18 million, of which $11 million went on building costs and the remainder on new telephone and reporting systems. The SFE wanted a world-class trading floor and so it commissioned the Chicago-based Glenn Windstrup as project consultant. Windstrup had retired and was running a bicycle shop when Hosking contacted him. Hosking said:

> He was semi-retired, living in the western suburbs [of Chicago] but I convinced him to move to Australia for a year and help us build our exchange . . . I figured, why reinvent

Ranald Stewart, general manager of finance and administration at the SFE, dons a hard hat to survey progress at the site of the exchange's new home in Grosvenor Street.

the wheel? Why tamper with a concept that has proven wildly successful?

Windstrup, principal of Task Management Incorporated, had spent 25 years working for the Chicago Mercantile Exchange, where he had a major role in designing and installing the facilities of what is acknowledged as the world's best-designed exchange. Space Management Programmes Inc of Chicago, specialists in trading-floor design and architects of the CME's facilities (and consultants to the Chicago Board of Trade and Comex), were consulting architects to the local firm Inscan Design. The new trading floor, described by the SFE as 'unashamedly modelled on the best design features of the CME', occupied 9500 square feet, about three times the space available at 13–15 O'Connell Street.

Advanced technology was the hallmark of the new trading floor. The telephone system had 1200 phone lines connected to 200 dual-handset consoles (equivalent to 400 handsets) with each dual console catering for up to 60 lines; the system could be expanded to 480 dual consoles. The telephone exchange,

Grand new premises in the nineteenth-century historic Royal Naval House and Federation Hall which were gutted and renovated to accommodate the expanding and high-tech SFE.

owned and operated by the SFE, was modelled on a system installed in the New York Stock Exchange. A new computer system, owned and operated by the SFE, was installed to cope with price-reporting, trade-matching and telecommunications. For the previous eight years the price-reporting facilities had been provided under contract by AAP Reuters Information Services. With the development of the SFE's own price-reporting system, the exchange became a vendor as well as producer of price information, selling to data systems and news and wire services around the world. Huge growth in trading volumes and pressure to replace outmoded software led the exchange to follow the practice used in most major exchanges and introduce its own price-reporting and trade-matching system. Price-reporting and trade-entry staff were provided with a catwalk suspended above the trading floor, enabling them to see and hear clearly the activity in the pits. Price monitoring screens were suspended above the catwalk so that traders in the pits could see the latest price information. The trading booths were equipped with the latest in technology, including personal computers and a specialised phone system.

The Hon. Nick Greiner, Premier of NSW (left), opens the Grosvenor Street premises on 3 February 1989. With him are SFE chairman John Oliver (centre) and chief executive Les Hosking.

The modular design of the trading floor would allow pits to be reduced or expanded, or new pits to be added, as conditions changed. The trading floor was also equipped with a manual over-ride in the air-conditioning system so that if one pit's trading became frenzied its overheated occupants could be cooled down.

By early 1989 it had become known that the owners of ICCH—a group of major UK banks—were keen to wind back the clearing house's overseas commitments. And the SFE had its own plans. In March 1989 the exchange informed ICCH of its intention to move to self-clearing. A considerable amount of work lay ahead, with a number of alternatives to be examined, but the exchange was determined to take control of its own clearing procedures. Just how this would occur remained to be thrashed out.

The SFE's objective was to combine three features which few organisations could boast having under one roof: a self-regulating structure, a trading and price-reporting system and

The new trading floor at 31 Grosvenor Street, unashamedly modelled on the best design features of the Chicago Mercantile Exchange and including the latest in telephone and computer technology.

self-clearing. This would render the SFE a uniquely self-contained organisation in which counterparty risk would be minimised. Another stimulus to the move towards self-clearing was that while trading volumes on the SFE were consistently rising—the first five months of 1989 recorded 4.81 million contracts, 61 per cent up on the same period in 1988—floor members were suffering because of competitive fee-cutting. The growing volumes of trading on the SFE were disguising the cut-throat competition among brokers for business. It was estimated that some 65 per cent of the business was handled by the top 10 houses, so that many operators were not profitable. Self-clearing was widely regarded as providing some solution. However, smaller members of the SFE were concerned about having to find a minimum contribution of $1 million to a guarantee fund and a minimum net tangible asset backing of $2 million.

Celebrating the move to Grosvenor Street at a dinner at Darling Harbour: (left to right) SFE chief executive, Les Hosking; founding chairman, Clive Hall; and former chief executive David Rutledge.

In April, low activity in the eurodollar and T-bond LIFFE-linked futures forced the SFE to suspend trading in the two contracts. Similarly, lack of trading caused the SFE to decide, a couple of months later, to sever its link with Comex. The exchange was also examining an overhaul of the $A futures contract, which had not lived up to expectations and had traded poorly from the outset. And the exchange was being forced to consider the unthinkable: change the specifications of, or find a substitute for, a successful contract, the ten-year bond contract, ranked second most highly traded. The problem was that while bond futures were rising the number of physical bonds was contracting because the federal government had changed from deficit budgeting to operating with a surplus. The withdrawal of government borrowing put an end to new bond issues. The drop in the supply of the physical paper left the futures market vulnerable to price manipulation, as had been evidenced by an alleged squeeze in the September 1988 ten-year bond contract. The SFE responded by altering the method for obtaining the settlement price for

Top: *The latest in technology improves trading conditions and ensures swift and accurate reporting and confirmation of trades.* Below: *Traders enjoy the new trading floor, February 1989.*

February 1989: a busy month for the SFE when Sydney hosted the 1990s Asia–Pacific Futures Markets conference. Here a panel gives a northern hemisphere view of the Asia–Pacific region: (left to right) Michael Jenkins, chief executive of LIFFE; Bill Grossman, vice-president of the Chicago Board of Trade; Bill Brodsky, president and chief executive of the Chicago Mercantile Exchange; Gene Donney, president Elders Futures Inc; and (speaking) Dr Henry Jarecki, a member of the Comex board of governors.

the bond close-out, taking quotes relating to a wider spread of bonds to calculate the price.

Progress was achieved on two other fronts. In April 1989 the SFE announced that its electronic after-hours screen-dealing system, SYCOM, would begin operating later in the year. A new contract based on a semi-government bond was making its appearance after a two-year gestation period. The new contract, the first fixed-interest futures contract to be deliverable, began trading on 25 October 1989, at a time when conditions were volatile in the wake of Wall Street's mini-crash on Friday 13 October. Expectations were that the long-awaited semi-government futures contract would benefit from the increased turnover in physical semi-government bonds, which at that time was greater than trading in the ten-year commonwealth bonds. The SFE was working on two

Mrs Elizabeth Sam, chairman of Simex, was a speaker at the 1990s Asia–Pacific Futures Markets conference.

more contracts scheduled for the following year, one in equities and one dealing with currencies.

On 30 November, the SFE extended its trading hours and its international presence with the launch of SYCOM, which traded from 4.45pm until midnight. On the same day, LIFFE launched a new automated trading product, Automated Pit Trading, which operated from 4.30 to 6pm, extending trading by 90 minutes. SYCOM, based on a network of personal computers linked to a host computer, initially traded only ten-year commonwealth bonds but subsequently expanded to include all SFE contracts. Only SFE floor members were eligible to have SYCOM terminals; locals could have access for their own trading through a screen in their nominating floor member's office. SYCOM quickly proved popular as an after-hours automated trading system, providing access to its market when the trading floor was closed, with the SYCOM session treated as the first trading session of the following day. During 1989 the SFE was one of the first exchanges to signal its intention to join Globex—the after-hours screen-dealing system developed by the Chicago Mercantile Exchange, the Chicago Board of Trade and Reuters—which began trading in June 1992.

The year 1989 went down as another bumper period. Uncertainty about the direction of interest rates boosted turnover, which increased by 50 per cent on the previous year's

The Hon. John Fahey, MP, minister for employment and industrial relations and minister assisting the Premier, rings the bell to start trading in the semi-government futures contract, 25 October 1989.

7.5 million to 11.82 million. Trading in the bank-accepted bill futures had risen by 96 per cent to nearly six million contracts, putting it on par with the most liquid financial instrument futures anywhere in the world. Options on the bill futures contract had rocketed by 170 per cent. Trading in share-price index futures options had leaped by 80 per cent, compared with a mere 9.4 per cent rise in SPI futures trading. These results gave the SFE its seventh consecutive lift in annual turnover.

Towards the end of 1989 John Oliver retired after seven-and-a-half years as chairman. He could look back on the many objectives achieved: lifting the SFE's image, building its financial strength and promoting the strength of the exchange and its members internationally. Oliver had presided over a period of enormous growth, development and activity for the SFE. His breadth of contacts, in business and government, brought the exchange a huge advantage. Probably his chief contribution lay in the area of surveillance compliance. 'The

SFE chairman Bruce Hudson pushes the button to start trading on SYCOM, 30 November 1989.

self-regulation of the SFE owed a lot to John Oliver,' said Les Hosking. 'John took on the role of chairman of the committee of inspection and audit, one of the hardest jobs of all time.' Founding chairman of the CIA, Oliver continued as convenor of that committee as well as serving on several other exchange committees and on the SFE board.

By the time he relinquished the chairmanship, the SFE had developed a sound administrative structure and acquired senior staff with a deep knowledge of the industry. Later, Oliver described the role of chairman as 'part pusher, part investigator, part passenger', adding, 'sometimes it's quite hard to know which role to take'. He is remembered as a chairman who refrained from interfering except when he had something to contribute, a 'man of the people' who commanded respect while putting others at ease. Oliver was succeeded by Bruce Hudson, who had been deputy for five years and a board member since 1982. Eric Spooner, a director since 1983, became deputy chairman. The SFE, approaching its thirtieth birthday, could look back on several years of outstanding growth in trading and membership, and remarkable achievements in technology, regulation and business development. More achievements were to come—Les Hosking was still only halfway through the five-year plan he had begun in 1988. But the next few years were to be more eventful than he realised.

8
Legislation: putting the house in order

While the changes embodied in the Rutledge and Hosking visions for the Sydney Futures Exchange were implemented one by one, and as new contracts and new technology extended the market's horizons, changes in industry regulation were also dramatically altering the world of futures.

Futures industry legislation had been needed long before it was introduced in 1986. Until then, the SFE could influence its own members but had no powers over 'fringe' operators. This had been a problem during the gold boom years when unsophisticated investors were tempted to trade futures contracts, and again in the early 1980s, the era of bucket shops, sham futures brokers and other shady businesses. While operating outside the SFE, they adversely affected the image of futures trading and the exchange. The losses by Australian investors through bucket shops such as the leveraged currency operators between 1983 and 1986 ran into millions of dollars. In contrast to the reluctance it had displayed when regulations were virtually thrust upon it in the form of the 1979 NSW legislation, the exchange was coming to realise that it could benefit from legislation, particularly in view of the shift in favour of financial futures and the internationalisation that came in the 1980s.

The exchange began operating in 1960 with articles and by-laws broadly based on those of the London market. The exchange's articles basically regulated the behaviour of members and the by-laws set out the terms of the contracts traded in markets operated by the exchange. With the passage of time, and with several revisions, the articles came to cover the behaviour of members in their relationships first with the exchange, second with other members and, ultimately, with their clients. The SFE was rewriting its regulations as early as the late 1960s, prompted by the knowledge that if it did not take the initiative, this would be seized by the state government through its Corporate Affairs Commission (CAC). From that time the exchange had considerable input from the law firm Laurence & Laurence, with first Nigel Mainwaring, then James Williams and later John Currie regularly attending board meetings. The lawyers would often return to their offices laden with exchange-related work after lengthy SFE board meetings.

In its early days, the philosophy of the exchange was very much influenced by the UK view that too much regulation was not to be encouraged because it could stifle a market. Members' obligations to each other, to the clearing house and to their clients were understood and performed in a fairly genteel and club-like but professional atmosphere. This self-regulatory regime prevailed fairly satisfactorily for a number of years. However, it was later to prove inadequate, particularly in the late 1970s and early 1980s, when the clientele of the SFE underwent significant change as members began dealing with a broader public and the exchange's membership itself radically altered to include some far brasher operators than were ever found among the wooltraders.

The exchange's articles and by-laws were amended at various times but the first formal legislation to affect its operations, the NSW Futures Markets Act, was drawn up in 1979. This act, which came into force on 14 December, was enacted by the NSW parliament and applied only in that state. Its provisions were mostly based on the securities industry legislation introduced in 1970. The NSW Futures Markets Act 1979 was drafted to enable the cash-settled currency futures contracts to be launched. Prevailing foreign-exchange controls prohibited such a contract being written in a foreign currency because delivery of the contract would not be possible, so contracts resulting in delivery had to be cash-settled in Australian dollars. This raised the issue of whether the cash-settled currency futures contracts could be struck down as illegal under the provisions of the NSW Gaming and Betting Act 1912, on the grounds that such a cash-settlement procedure left the contract more or less equivalent to a bet. The uncertainty was not over whether one opinion was right and one wrong; the question had to be resolved to achieve a degree of commercial certainty. And so the SFE approached the NSW government with a request that the contract should be exempted from the provisions of the Gaming and Betting Act. At a subsequent meeting between Ralph Watzlaff, then deputy principal solicitor of the CAC, and NSW Treasury's Jim Watt, four alternatives were outlined:

- to do nothing;
- to give the SFE an exemption from the Gaming and Betting Act;
- to give an exemption but retain some oversight; or
- to launch a full-blown US-style Commodity and Futures Trading Commission regulatory regime.

The view of the CAC, put forward by Watzlaff, was that the third option offered the best balance, combining an exemption from the Gaming and Betting Act with some supervision of the futures market, such as the ability to examine SFE rules and to require that the SFE notify the NSW Attorney-General of any changes to be made to the rules. The CAC was not anxious to assume any greater degree of control. Legislation was prepared on this basis. Watzlaff recalled: 'A couple of politicians were quite resistant to the idea that the government was doing anything at all to support the futures industry. The image of the industry was not good in those days.' However, it was accepted that it was in the public interest to have as wide as possible a range of risk-management techniques. 'It was not a matter of judging whether futures were a good or bad idea,' said Watzlaff. 'The issue was broader. The government wanted to support the SFE as part of a move to establish Sydney as a finance centre offering a range of risk-management tools to business and industry.' With this in mind, a wider range of contracts offered by a stronger futures exchange would be a welcome initiative.

The SFE was less than pleased to discover legislation was

looming and was vigorously opposed to being bracketed with the stock exchange under securities industry legislation. An early concern was that the securities industry legislation would be applied to futures trading entirely and without modification. This worry receded as the differences between the two industries were emphasised. The SFE pointed out that there was no parallel in a stock exchange for futures industry features such as the legal nexus between the clearing house and the exchange, margin calls and the exchange's legal relationship not just with a handful of floor members but hundreds of associate members. Futures industry representatives—Clive Hall, Desmond Brook and Pat Nicholas from the exchange, and Jim Sinclair from ICCH—turned up in NSW parliament to hear the bill go through its second reading in November 1979. The act set down an important definition: 'For the purpose of any Act or law, a futures contract made at a futures market maintained by a futures exchange is not a contract by way of gaming or wagering.'

The act went further than merely granting the exemption sought by the SFE, in that it introduced a degree of regulation over the activities of the exchange. This caused trouble. Those drafting the NSW legislation had assumed that Treasury would keep the SFE informed of progress. This had not been the case. To the CAC's surprise, the SFE was incensed at what the commission had thought was a laudable effort. The regulation that the SFE would have to submit its rules to the NSW Attorney-General, and that the NSW government had the power to disallow an amendment to an SFE rule, ruffled the exchange, which felt it should have been consulted. The SFE made no formal complaint but set about discussing some amendments to be made to the legislation and began revising and reworking its own articles and by-laws to substantially improve its self-regulatory procedures. The episode, however, brought the SFE into closer contact with the CAC and encouraged further moves to improve the protection of members, their clients and thus the market.

The exchange's new articles and by-laws, drawn up over about eighteen months, were largely the work of a committee chaired by Desmond Brook and including David Rutledge, Dick Newman and Les Hosking (then with ICCH), working with Nigel Mainwaring and James Williams of Laurence &

Laurence. The new regulations, which went through some twenty drafts and various negotiations with the CAC, secured approval from the state legislators in June 1981. The articles were adopted by SFE members at a general meeting in October 1981 and took effect from 1 February 1982. The objective was to confer a more conservative image on futures trading in Australia. A significant advance was the provision of greater protection for the general public. A committee of inspection and audit was established with the power to examine the financial affairs of exchange members and to monitor their activities to ensure they complied with the new rules. The SFE board was to include two independent directors, enhancing objective scrutiny of the exchange's operations. Members were required to maintain records of instructions from clients and to use a standard form of client agreement specified by the exchange. Members were also required to place surplus client funds with either ICCH or another approved corporation; in particular, it was forbidden for members to use such funds to finance their own trading or that of other clients. The practice of calling deposits and margins from clients was made compulsory. This was to lessen the risk that a broker might fail and was thus additional protection for clients; until then brokers (floor and associate members) were required to call deposits from clients but margin-calling was not compulsory between broker and client, so that sometimes a broker would meet an ICCH call for margins (which had to be paid) but not in turn call the funds from the client. Further, no client was to be allowed to dominate a broker's business to the point where the client's business impaired the broker's ability to meet its obligations. And brokers were to put client business ahead of their own. The new articles also ensured that members kept proper accounts and filed quarterly financial returns with the SFE. Associate members dealing with the public came under obligations similar to those applying to floor members. Floor members dealing with the public had to maintain a minimum net tangible asset backing of $100 000; a minimum NTA of $50 000 applied to associate members. The new rules also prescribed standards for advertising. Clive Hall, serving his fourth term as SFE chairman and by then planning to retire, believed the tougher rules would usher in a new era for the Sydney Futures

Exchange. Hall was quoted in *The Australian Financial Review*, 15 May 1981:

> We are most anxious to introduce the new articles because we feel they will offer a greater degree of protection for the public wishing to engage in futures trading . . . [The committee of inspection and audit] will have the power to make random inquiries into the financial affairs of all members, a practice which is widely used overseas to protect the public from brokers who may overextend themselves . . . I believe that providing outside directors with no financial interest in the marketplace will give the public and business community generally a lot more confidence in futures trading . . . Most of the problems have been experienced by associate members and with the new rules we will have better control of their activities.

The new rules were a vast improvement on the earlier regime but deficiencies remained. During the early 1980s momentum began to build for national legislation, driven by episodes such as that involving Southern Cross, the failure of some SFE members and the early bucket-shop activities. Support for the legislation came from a range of sources: the Campbell Committee, which in 1981 had turned in a landmark report on the Australian financial system favouring, among other initiatives, increased investor protection through legislation; the NCSC; the judiciary; and the SFE. Proposals for national legislation were heard from 1983 but nothing formal was established until the following year, when the NSW CAC put forward a proposal outlining a far broader form of regulation than had hitherto been in place. This tied together material from a series of member problems and failures and, among other features, required market participants to be licensed, supported the concept of segregated accounts for clients' funds and stipulated that proper accounts must be kept. A fidelity fund or some form of insurance provision was also proposed. These suggestions were approved. The states agreed to a new Futures Industry Code, which would form part of the cooperative scheme administered by the NCSC and its delegates, the state CACs. This was a victory for those keen to see the futures industry adopt a more ethical and professional approach to customer protection.

National legislation was beginning to take shape. The

smaller states had little interest and most of the work was handled by NSW, Victoria and Queensland. The commonwealth parliamentary council became involved in 1984/85 in drafting the final document. In 1984 a first draft was sent out for comment; the SFE and ICCH responded with their submissions. A second exposure draft was circulated in 1985 and drew further responses. In August 1985 representatives from all states gathered on Hamilton Island in the Barrier Reef to tidy up outstanding issues.

Changes drafted in the mid-1980s placed even greater emphasis on client protection with provisions that severely curtailed the potential for fraud. And the rules were widened to apply to members' activities generally; for example, when they traded on overseas exchanges.

By this time, in the mid-1980s, the SFE was raising its international profile. Work was under way to establish links with New York's Comex and LIFFE in London and deregulation of Australian financial markets had enabled greater overseas participation in SFE markets. Rutledge, influenced in favour of stronger regulation by his US experience, was enthusiastic. Some at the SFE had not been supportive of the new legislation but that changed as the exchange forged ahead with its internationalisation.

An incentive in the mid-1980s for establishing a tougher regulatory framework was mounting concern about the activities of bucket shops, which flourished from 1983 to 1986. They operated outside of SFE control but the SFE was damned by association because the bucket shops claimed to deal in 'futures contracts'. The bucket shops came in various guises, from leveraged currency operations to Malaysian red-bean dealers, all tempting unwary or greedy speculators. Many made false and misleading assertions in their advertising, one promising 175 per cent returns on investments. The bucket shops were not caught by 1979 NSW legislation because they were not members of the exchange. However, one South-East Asian organisation, G.H. Shintoh Australia Ltd, had taken out associate membership to provide a facade of respectability through its SFE trading. The SFE and the CAC were able to act once the Futures Code came into effect because it forced Shintoh to bring its overseas operations under its licence and SFE membership. Enormous effort went into the investigation of the Shintoh group and the subsequent trials and convictions for fraud; investigations into the group were carried out in Victoria and South Australia, with the Victorian CAC sending agents to Malaysia and Taiwan. Shintoh was ultimately expelled from the exchange. The SFE also lent its support to a clean-up operation to eliminate leveraged currency broking by making its own investigations and advising the CAC. No SFE members were involved in leveraged currency broking, which the SFE regarded as another form of undesirable off-market trading.

The legislation that came into force on 1 July 1986 put the lid on the bucket shops' business. It required that all futures trading had to be conducted on a futures market by licensed persons who were members of the SFE or of another self-regulated organisation. Within two weeks of the new legislation being in place, the NSW CAC took action against Shoreline Currencies (Australia) Pty Ltd, following complaints from investors alleging they had been misled. Shoreline's advertisements were very seductive, even suggesting that 88 per cent of their clients could earn a profit of 104 per cent a year. As well as investigating Shoreline, the NSW CAC was looking into the activities of other companies offering similar schemes, including Currency Brokers (Australia) Pty Ltd, Consolidated Currencies Pty Ltd, Carragreen Currencies Corporation Pty Ltd, Lombard Nash International Pty Ltd and Octile Pty Ltd. By late 1986 some 25 leveraged currency operators were under CAC investigation. The CAC was successful in a number of actions, following a test case in which Carragreen's activities were found to be in breach of the Futures Industry Code and the Companies Code.

The Futures Industry Act was replaced in 1991 by the Futures Industry Chapter of the Corporations Act, administered by the Australian Securities Commission and known as the Futures Law. The Futures Law imposes a number of obligations on futures brokers, such as maintaining clients' funds and other client property separately from the broker's own funds in a segregated account and adhering to strict rules concerning payments and withdrawals from these accounts. Documents covering clients' trading must be regularly prepared and provided to clients, detailing each futures or option transaction, along with monthly statements. Brokers must keep comprehensive records of transactions dealt for themselves or on behalf of related companies. The law also stipulates that brokers must observe regulations prohibiting market manipulation and artificial price-making, false trading and market rigging.

All futures markets must be maintained on approved futures exchanges and all futures trading for clients must occur either on a local approved futures exchange or an overseas recognised futures exchange that is specified in the regulations. Further, a futures market is defined as a market, exchange or other place at which, or a facility by means of which, futures contracts are regularly made. The definition has been held to be wide enough to catch activities such as those of leveraged currency dealers who were regarded as conducting an illegal futures market. The Futures Law also tries to define a futures market by reference to features that distinguish futures trading from other forms of commodity trading, especially those involving forward trading. Under the Futures Law, a futures exchange must have ministerial approval.

The legislation required a further major revision of the SFE's articles and by-laws. It also obliged the SFE to establish a fidelity fund, to cover financial losses to clients resulting from defalcation or fraudulent misuse of money or other property. The fund would be available in a case where, say, an employee of an exchange member misused a client's money and the member was unable to reimburse the client. The fund would not be available to compensate for market losses or a member's negligence. The SFE's board could use its discretion in the case of a substantial financial shortfall caused by a major client default. The SFE contributed an initial $500 000 and members contributed by way of a levy on trades. The fidelity fund is administered by a management committee of the exchange.

The SFE's regulations reinforce many of the provisions of the legislation and provide a detailed code of conduct for members. The exchange's business rules impose additional obligations on members who deal with clients:

- floor members must maintain minimum net tangible assets of

$A1 million; full associate members must have $250 000 in net tangible assets and introducing broker associates $50 000;

- members must complete and lodge quarterly financial statements;
- members must execute a written client agreement with every client containing the minimum details as determined by the exchange;
- members must ensure that initial margins are called from clients regarding all futures and options positions;
- members must call for a variation margin payment from a client when that client's net debit margin exceeds 25 per cent of the total initial margin;
- where a margin call has not been satisfied by a client within five business days the member must 'top up' the client's segregated account by a deposit of its own funds.

The SFE's committee for inspection and audit, and its compliance and surveillance staff, are responsible for ensuring that the Futures Law and the SFE's business rules are followed. The SFE's business rules cover dispute arbitration to provide an impartial method of settling disputes between members, and between members and clients, where the parties are unable to resolve the matters. This offers a swifter and less expensive alternative to court proceedings.

As the exchange's activities expanded, specific trading etiquette had to be devised for SYCOM and new rules approved for the Sydney Futures Exchange Clearing House (SFECH). With existing rules in the US and UK as a guide, the planners—the SFE, notably its in-house lawyer Tony Dreise, its legal and accounting advisers and outside consultant Ian McGaw—were able to put together the clearing house's legal structure within twelve months.

Few major problems have occurred since the Futures Law came into force. Surveillance is tighter but breaches have not entirely been eliminated. In some instances, market manipulation has been alleged in the bond futures contract. The NCSC held an inquiry into the settlement of the September 1988 ten-year bond futures contract following concerns that dominant positions in the physical market had been used to affect the market. The SFE's response was to alter the method for determining a settlement price for the bond close-out.

Until then, ICCH would ask twelve major bond dealers for their prices for relevant bonds, drop the highest and lowest quotes and take an average of the remaining ten, which would be the settlement price. This was changed so that an average price was derived from quotes for a basket of at least three series of highly liquid bonds. Another episode, involving substantial buying in the physical market a short time ahead of the June 1990 three-year bond close-out, was investigated by the SFE and resulted in another change. Settlement procedures were altered so that bond prices were obtained from the market not once but three times during the morning of settlement day, thus substantially diminishing the possible impact on settlement prices of significant cash-market trading.

With national futures legislation, its own vastly extended business rules, in-house legal counsel and upgraded emphasis on compliance, the SFE has come a long way from operating with a set of rules it drafted and policed itself.

9
Encounters with ICCH, fighting with FOX

When Les Hosking originally conceived his ambition that the Sydney Futures Exchange would take over its own clearing functions, his hope was that the change would coincide with the exchange's move to new premises in Grosvenor Street and the upgrading of its computer systems. However, the SFE did not want to overextend itself by trying to do too much too quickly. Nor did it want to sever connections with ICCH until an adequate substitute was established.

Hosking had known that from the mid-1980s, and particularly in the aftermath of the October 1987 stockmarket crash, the London exchanges were increasingly concerned about the offshore commitments of UK banks—the owners of ICCH. The banks themselves finally decided that they would rather not be in the business of extending guarantees to overseas exchanges. The clearing-house guarantee operates like a last-resort facility for market participants should a member default on a contract. While ICCH was under increasing pressure to shed its obligations in Australia, it did not want to be seen as walking away from its responsibilities. Ideally, it would have liked to shed the guarantee but continue to provide lucrative fee-earning services. The UK chairman of ICCH, John Berkshire, had visited Australia during the mid-1980s and had indicated that it was likely that ICCH's services might not be available to the SFE for much longer. The UK banks were anxious to see ICCH's guarantee confined to the London exchanges. Reservations about the guarantee existed on both sides, with the SFE for its part concerned that Sydney could wake up one morning and find the funds gone because ICCH's guarantee operated on a basis of first come, first served and it covered a number of exchanges. With unease about the guarantee considerably intensified after the crash, Berkshire, again in Australia, made plain to the SFE's John Oliver and Bruce Hudson that ICCH's plan was to give the SFE the required twelve months' notice in 1991. Hudson recalled coming away from the meeting feeling 'quite concerned'.

The SFE's steering committee on clearing, chaired by Hudson, had voted to proceed towards self-clearing. But the SFE had to secure 75 per cent support from members before it could give ICCH the requisite twelve months' formal notice of termination (although in fact the board had the power to act without the required level of member approval). Gaining the 75 per cent approval from members proved to be a significant obstacle: the SFE's floor members were far from being a united body, with some strenuously opposed to a split from ICCH, some worried about funding a new guarantee and others viewing self-clearing as a financial bonanza. Hosking was among those who coveted ICCH's healthy earnings in Australia—all of which sprang from servicing the growing volumes traded on the SFE.

ICCH, perhaps unrealistically, remained hopeful that it would retain this income from computer and management services, while the SFE would take over the burden of the guarantee. But the clearing house was growing impatient with the SFE's failure to come up with firm proposals. Impatience turned to mutual animosity. The dispute, involving countless meetings between representatives of the two organisations, dragged on for more than a year. For ICCH, the uncertainty over an eventual resolution brought problems in staffing, planning and morale. For the exchange, the situation was a frustrating impasse, with the membership bogged down in indecision. For Bruce Hudson and Les Hosking it was a period of meeting upon meeting with floor members. Getting together at least twice with each member lifted the level of contact between members and the exchange's chairman and chief executive in a way that was probably quite beneficial for the SFE.

In June 1990 a barrier fell: the SFE floor members approved a decision to form a wholly-owned subsidiary, Sydney Futures Exchange Clearing House (SFECH), to clear and guarantee contracts traded on the SFE, with a view to the new arrangements coming into place on 1 December 1991. The members resolutely refused to go so far as approving the termination of arrangements with ICCH, but planning committees could go ahead with vital measures including securing approval from the Australian Securities Commission and the Trade Practices Commission for the clearing rules, forming a guarantee facility of $A100 million and integrating new clearing, processing and risk-analysis systems into the existing computer facilities. ICCH had still not formally been given notice.

In October 1990, ICCH took the initiative away from the exchange. It gave notice that, from 30 November 1991, it would no longer be providing clearing and guaranteeing facilities to the SFE. ICCH was in fact doing the SFE a favour, removing the need to secure 75 per cent agreement from members before giving notice to ICCH. Any satisfaction the SFE might have felt was short-lived. ICCH dropped a bombshell by putting to SFE members proposals for an alternative clearing house that offered wider membership. The SFE had antagonised associate members and some floor members by proposing that only floor members would have access to its new clearing house. The SFE, rocked by ICCH's alternative, responded by amending its plans to make them more appealing to members and associates.

The SFE forged ahead with its plan while the ICCH alternative remained a background threat. The project absorbed enormous resources in terms of research and development. SFECH was incorporated on 9 November as a separate legal entity with its own board but as a wholly-owned subsidiary of the SFE. In modelling the structure and procedures of SFECH on clearing-house arrangements in the US, the SFE was following a worldwide trend towards increasingly standardised futures trading systems, a decision that would simplify access to the SFE for foreigners. The establishment of SFECH was also a reflection of the SFE's determination to 'Australianise' clearing arrangements to ensure the continued health and integrity of the Australian futures industry. The SFE believed that a wholly-owned clearing house should be supported by the financial commitment of its clearing members and be fully integrated with the exchange, with input and access to the exchange risk-management programs and other computer systems. SFECH was to begin operations formally on 1 December 1991. Meanwhile, ICCH would continue to serve the SFE, the mutual hostility deferring to the imperatives of business.

The SFE put its clearing house together in twelve months—staffing, finding $100 million for the guarantee, getting members prepared for the new system. 'We did in twelve months what would normally take three years,' said Hosking. 'The brawl with ICCH delayed our plans.'

Early in December 1990 the SFE issued a 'final document' outlining the structure of a clearing house and incorporating substantial revisions of earlier proposals, especially regarding what was required of clearing members and how they would be remunerated. Clearing membership of the SFE would be open to any floor or associate member of the exchange with a net tangible asset backing of $2 million. Clearing members would provide a minimum contribution of $1 million (with an additional amount varying with the member's open positions) to the $100 million clearing guarantee which was to be composed of $5 million from the SFE, $45 million from clearing members and $50 million from an external insurer. Clearing fees would remain at 32 cents a side (64 cents a round turn). The SFE decided against paying clearing members a dividend but instead would reimburse them for the risk undertaken through an accommodation fee of a minimum of 1 per cent a quarter (4 per cent a year) of each member's guarantee commitment. An additional discretionary fee would be determined periodically.

In February 1991 the SFE was declared the winner of the race to establish a new clearing house. ICCH—by then renamed the London Clearing House—announced that it would not be 'proactive' in promoting its alternative clearing arrangements, although it would continue to develop the idea.

The necessary member commitments were obtained early in 1991, before SFECH began operating. In October of that year SFECH welcomed its first overseas member when Cargill

Investor Services (CIS), one of the world's top ten futures and options broking houses, announced it had joined forces with the local futures broker C.A. & L. Bell Commodities to become a clearing member. CIS was the first overseas, non-bank group to commit itself as a member of SFECH and its announcement was a major boost for the credibility of the new clearing house. SFECH rapidly acquired membership commitments from 26 organisations, including leading banks from the UK, US, Germany and Switzerland.

In what Hosking called a 'major landmark in the SFE's thirty-year history', the exchange on 1 December 1991 took over responsibility for clearing and guaranteeing its markets through its wholly-owned subsidiary. It was a signal of the completion of the SFE's five-year development program which included moving to new premises in February 1989, introducing after-hours screen-dealing with SYCOM and installing the latest fully integrated computer systems for price-reporting, trade-matching, surveillance and clearing. During 1991 the exchange added a clearing and processing system to be used by SFECH, and an on-line confirmation and allocation system, STACS (Sydney Trade Allocation and Confirmation System), providing instantaneous confirmation. STACS provided the SFE with one of the most efficient trade-clearance systems in the world. The result has been a fully integrated system which enables efficient recording and reporting of trades and registration and clearing of contracts traded either on the floor, screen or off-exchange. In the 1991 annual report, Les Hosking commented:

> Without a doubt, the most significant development in the history of the Exchange has been the move to self-clearing . . . There is no doubt that the considerable investment made by the Exchange in technology in trading and clearing will benefit the Members and their clients in increased efficiency of existing markets and ability to facilitate further growth in those markets and new markets.

Hosking had always been confident that the exchange would have its own clearing house and he was the passionate driving force behind the project. Much of the credit was also awarded to Glenn Windstrup, who triumphed over time to get computer facilities in place.

Thirtieth anniversary dinner, Sheraton Wentworth Hotel, Sydney. The Hon. Nick Greiner, Premier of NSW, delivers a keynote speech.

After several years of spectacular growth in trading, 1990—the year that marked the SFE's thirtieth anniversary—was a period of consolidation. Contracts traded declined by 3 per cent from 1989's hefty volumes, a trend that was not unique to Australia, but trading was active in the lead-up to the Australian federal election in March 1990. The 90-day bank-accepted bill futures contract hit a record volume of 76 396 on 15 February, a day that also saw record overall turnover of 129 603 contracts. After the election conditions were calmer, with the government's tight monetary policy leading to a general slowdown in trading that persisted throughout the year. Financial markets activity generally was dampened by a contraction in trading limits and in the number of operators (mostly because of mergers or closures), and this was reflected in lower trading volumes. The SFE responded to the recessionary conditions by reducing staff and holding expenditure in check. A bright note was a sustained increase in SYCOM's daily volumes, which rose from 393 at the start of the year to a peak of 943 in November 1990, a month when the decline

SFE chairman Bruce Hudson (front, left of centre) hosts guests at the SFE's 30th anniversary dinner. Clockwise from Hudson: Bob King, chairman of ICCH; Clive Hall; Kevin Troy, ASX; Bill Robinson, NCSC; Jim Watt, NSW Treasury Corporation; John Phillips, deputy governor of the Reserve Bank of Australia; and the Hon. Nick Greiner, Premier of NSW.

in trading volumes generally was reversed. Trading in SYCOM hit a record of 20 744 contracts for the month. Growth was strongest in the interest-rate contracts: 90-day bank-accepted bills increased in activity by 48 per cent in November compared with October, ten-year commonwealth bonds recorded a 56 per cent rise and trading in options on these bonds rose by 111 per cent.

With the Australian federal government continuing to run a budget surplus, and a fall-off in commonwealth bond activity, the SFE was keen to launch the revamped semi-government contracts. A deliverable semi-government contract had been introduced in October 1989 but with minimal success, and the exchange was now looking at devising two semi-government contracts, of five and ten years, that would be cash-settled. While no new products were introduced during 1990, planning intensified for 1991 and beyond. The SFE entered 1991 with three goals in sight: introducing three new contracts—semi-government bond, equity index

A crowded and active trading floor on the night of the August 1990 budget—another busy evening trading session for the SFE.

and a new wool contract; establishing new clearing arrangements; and extending SYCOM for the full period between trading-floor sessions to provide 24-hour trading.

Then came a challenging, but ironic, development: more than thirty years after being launched as the Sydney Greasy Wool Futures Exchange, the SFE was now dusting off its agricultural files. The suspension of the reserve price scheme in February 1991 had ended price support for wool and raised the possibility of a revival of wool futures trading. The SFE began examining alternatives for a new wool contract.

International recognition of the SFE's achievements was increasing. The SFE received an international accolade when London Futures and Options Exchange (FOX) introduced its FAST system using technology based on the SFE's SYCOM. The prestige *Chicago Tribune*, in an article published on 18 February, described the Sydney exchange as one that 'many believe is the world's most completely equipped'. In the following month, the SFE's entry to the field of risk-management systems was vindicated when the world's third-largest futures exchange—the New York Mercantile Exchange (NYMEX), which boasts the largest turnover in fuel and other energy-based futures and option contracts—adopted an electronic screen-dealing system based on SYCOM. The system was chosen from a range of fiercely competing international risk-management systems. This had the potential to generate royalty payments for the SFE for its role in developing the system with Task Management Inc, a US-based software house specialising in software for derivative products.

Another milestone was the completion in March of the second generation of SYCOM. The system was expanded to provide access for up to 100 screens and permit trading in 1000 contract months and option strike prices. SYCOM's trading hours were extended from 4.40pm until 2am (later 4am) on all SFE contracts.

Meanwhile, there were disappointments: the recently listed five and ten-year semi-government bond futures contracts failed to flourish and the exchange delisted what seemed to have become doomed initiatives. That setback was offset by a sharp rise in trading volumes in May, largely on the back of news that the Australian inflation rate was falling significantly and that interest rates were falling further. On 16 May the SFE turned in a record morning session of 95 000 contracts, a number which rose to 127 000 by the close of business, one of the highest daily turnovers. Futures and option contracts traded in May totalled 1.2 million, almost 22 per cent more than a year earlier. At the end of the month politics pushed activity—the then Treasurer Paul Keating's unsuccessful challenge to Prime Minister Bob Hawke created an atmosphere of nervousness and hectic trading on SYCOM, with 9615 contracts dealt on the night of 30 May. That outdid a previous record of 3493 in September 1990. Volatility continued in June, with a new record daily average of nearly 70 000 contracts, but eased in July.

In August 1991 the SFE turned in a new and unscheduled direction when it launched a surprise bid for the New Zealand Futures and Options Exchange (NZFOE). The bid was in competition with London FOX, which had been negotiating to buy NZFOE and whose $NZ5.5 million (about $A4.2 million) offer was favoured by the sixteen members of the New Zealand exchange. For a year the NZFOE had been looking for a 'big brother' to whom to sell its business, driven by a need for access to a wider range of products that would be offered by a larger profit-oriented exchange. The NZ development had not been part of Hosking's strategic plan. Initially there had seemed to be no sound reason to buy the NZFOE but, during a stopover in Auckland, Hosking talked with the exchange's executives and, after doing some arithmetic, became convinced that there could be profit in the acquisition. Further benefits could flow from the fact that eight of NZFOE's sixteen members were also SFE members. The likelihood of a good return on the investment decided the SFE to make its last-minute offer, which was regarded by the NZFOE as a hostile bid and won support from a mere handful of the membership. Bids for the NZFOE had officially closed on 2 August, but the SFE, having sent a preliminary proposal, asked the board of the NZ exchange to allow its members to examine the SFE's full submission, completed on 23 August. Hosking said the SFE was 'very conscious of the timing' but emphasised that the Sydney exchange's bid focused on the common ground between the two exchanges. The SFE offered $NZ1.5 million upfront and $NZ4.5 million as incentive payments if NZ contracts met objectives over the coming three years.

The London exchange denounced the SFE's late bid, claiming it was a 'spoiling tactic'. An association with London FOX would lead to an internationalisation of NZFOE business, it said, whereas a merger with the SFE would leave it as a mere branch office of a regional exchange. At the end of August the board of the NZFOE recommended acceptance of London FOX's offer. The decision rested with the sixteen members, who had been given full details and an independent appraisal of the SFE proposal. Negotiations and discussions continued. London FOX set a 9 October deadline for acceptance of its bid. In mid-September the SFE presented two separate offers to the NZFOE, one bidding for shares in the exchange and a second bidding only for its business, and early in October the SFE altered its bid again to one that sought the business activities of the NZFOE and not the shareholdings. This was an important variation. The NZFOE had several court cases pending and the SFE's legal advisers had recommended buying the business and leaving the corporation. Any parties which sued would bring their actions against the corporation and the new entity which assumed the business would not be liable.

Then events took an unexpected turn. The NZFOE was forced to postpone the meeting at which a choice was to be made between the two competing bids. 'Irregularities' had emerged in London FOX's property futures trading and the exchange's chairman and its chief executive suddenly resigned. It was alleged that the exchange had been providing financial assistance to commodity brokers trading in its contracts, thereby boosting trading volumes, and offering other financial incentives to push new products. The controversy surrounding London FOX looked like putting it out of the race for the NZFOE. However, that did not signal plain sailing for the SFE. Resistance within the NZFOE membership to the Sydney bid could not be discounted. If the London FOX bid were removed, and the Sydney bid rejected, the move to sell NZFOE could well have to be shelved until an acceptable party showed interest. (OM International, the Stockholm Options Market, was one foreign organisation that had earlier been seriously interested in buying the NZ exchange.) By late October the SFE was back at the drawing board, modifying technical aspects of its offer. The sceptics at NZFOE, who had believed earlier that the SFE's bid was a purely defensive tactic that would be withdrawn in the absence of a rival for the region's business, admitted that they were becoming favourably impressed by the Sydney exchange's persistence. By 22 October, London FOX was officially out of the running, with the NZFOE board withdrawing its recommendation and members rejecting the bid. But the Sydney offer was still no more than under consideration. Discussions continued, with Hosking hopeful of a conclusion within a month or so. The NZFOE's chief executive, Len Ward, was reported in *The Australian Financial Review* as saying that if the SFE's best offer was not acceptable to shareholders, other options for restructuring the NZ exchange would be considered. Ward said that the two groups disagreed on a number of issues, one being a restraint-of-trade clause in the SFE's offer. According to Ward, the clause was 'not a major stumbling block to negotiations' but the concept was 'generally felt to be inappropriate in a free market which is what we are trying to achieve'. The SFE regarded the point as an important one; with 'restraint-of-trade' the NZFOE, with NZ$1.5 million from the SFE, could not set up a new and competing exchange.

An NZFOE board meeting on 22 November voted in favour of the SFE's bid and gave notice of an extraordinary general meeting of shareholders on 23 December. Months of haggling ended when the meeting accepted the SFE's $NZ6 million offer. An agreement was signed to the effect that the SFE acquired the business of NZFOE, with the NZ exchange becoming a wholly-owned unit of the SFE but retaining its name and operating with its own management and board. ICCH would continue to clear and guarantee for the NZFOE under an existing contract.

SFE turnover was at record levels as 1991 drew to a close. The economic and political uncertainties in Australia, together with the extraordinary events during the year, beginning with the Gulf war and ending with the break up of the Soviet Union, created volatility and uncertainty which brought a strong focus on risk management. The surge of activity underscored the exchange's role in enabling companies, financial institutions and individuals to hedge against risk—and produced the highest annual turnover in the SFE's history, at 12.49 million contracts. An increase of 8 per cent over 1990, this surpassed the previous record of 11.83 million contracts traded in 1989 and was in contrast to the downtrend in many of the world's futures and options exchanges. Options were a major contributor to SFE volume, increasing 26.5 per cent over the previous year's levels and representing 13.9 per cent of total turnover. Turnover in three-year and ten-year commonwealth bonds rose 31 per cent and 14 per cent, with bond options rising by 42 per cent and 31 per cent. The daily average of contracts traded in 1991 was 49 405, more than double the daily average of 22 072 traded four years earlier, before the launch of SYCOM. Such volumes would not be possible without the upgrading in computer systems that had taken place. While turnover was rising, the board was keeping a tight grip on budgets, conscious that financial markets were not as robust as they had been in the 1980s. The injection of resources into systems and computers continued.

At the end of 1991 Hosking embarked on another three-year plan, this time focusing on fine-tuning the exchange's facilities for over-the-counter traders. Also under discussion was the question of broadening the clearing activities of SFECH. This reflected Hosking's conviction that cross-clearing—having a clearing house register, margin and clear for several markets—would become a reality. 'It is beneficial from the point of view of capital adequacy, credit and regulatory oversight,' he said.

The opening of 1992 brought the launch of a new contract, the Fifty Leaders Index (FLI), based on the Australian Stock Exchange's Fifty Leaders share-price index. The index represents the 'blue-chips' and about 75 per cent of the market capitalisation of all stocks. FLI began trading on 29 January with initial trading boosted by a market-making scheme involving four SFE floor members and three locals. Each market-maker was required to quote five-point spreads on at least five lots when requested and consistently trade twenty or more contracts a day. The spirited trading across the futures markets continued in January—normally a quiet period—when the SFE produced another record monthly volume of 1.6 million contracts. Hosking remarked that Australian financial markets had a lot to digest: a new prime minister, following Keating's successful challenge to Hawke, the lowest inflation rate since 1964, uncertainty over interest rates which had been falling for two years, a 6 per cent plunge in the $A and an important economic package to be announced shortly by the federal government. 'This adds up to a volatile economic environment enabling a greater reliance on the futures markets as a medium for fast and effective risk management,' he said.

Hosking drew attention to the role of wool futures in risk management at an Agricultural Outlook conference in Canberra in February 1992. He said that the move towards deregulated commodity markets would necessitate the development of risk-management expertise in the agricultural sector, as it had done with corporates and financial institutions following financial deregulation. He pointed out that a large number of the wooltraders who had used wool futures in the 1970s and early 1980s had left the industry; consequently, the SFE was embarking on an extensive education program for the wool trade, growers and agricultural extension services.

Trading records continued to be broken as the use of futures increased. First-quarter volumes were up 50 per cent on the corresponding period in 1991. Trading in three-year bond futures rose by 187 per cent and in options on these bonds by 425 per cent. The release of the March 1992 quarter consumer price index figure, an unprecedented zero, took financial markets by surprise and triggered hectic trading on 29 April; 155 000 contracts were traded.

The increasing significance in the financial markets of managed futures funds in the early 1990s prompted the SFE to join the Managed Futures Association in the US and the European Managed Futures Association to gain a higher profile in both continents. In managed futures funds, professional advisers, managing their clients' assets on a discretionary basis, use futures markets as an investment tool. Their activity in SFE markets increased as managers looked for liquid futures contracts and options through which to spread their funds, a trend expected to continue.

In September 1992, Hosking affirmed that the SFE was still considerating joining Globex, although there were complications in reaching a decision. Globex, the computerised after-hours trading system owned by the Chicago futures exchanges and Reuters PLC, had been trading about 1000 contracts a night since it was launched in June 1992. Hosking favoured a link with Globex because it would bring trading opportunities for the futures community worldwide on to one screen. However, he pointed out that Sydney already had SYCOM and it was unrealistic to expect SFE members to lease expensive Globex computer terminals when Globex could be integrated with SYCOM. An article in the *Chicago Tribune*, 11 September, said that Hosking noted Sydney was not alone in this. 'Futures exchanges in London, Tokyo and Frankfurt are equipped with similar computerised trading systems and also might be reluctant to lease Globex terminals,' he said. 'Chicago is home to the world's two giant futures markets, and because of that fact, their leaders sometimes look inward.

The SFE board 1992 (left to right): Ken Connolly, John Oliver, Bruce Grant, chief executive Les Hosking, chairman Bruce Hudson, deputy chairman Peter Warne, Lewis Bell, Mark Cullen, Ron Thompson.

How to handle this question of leasing or using existing systems is just beginning to become a consideration for them.'

The exchange's success in technological development continued with the introduction in December 1992 of an innovative voice-recognition system that automatically took bids voiced by floor traders and recorded them on a computer which enabled instant worldwide access. Voice recognition replaced the earlier practice where dealers' messages were relayed to clerks who keyed the information into a computer. The new system, which brought greater accuracy in price reporting and a saving in costs, attracted considerable interest when it was demonstrated at a major conference on technology for financial markets held in October in Chicago. By early 1993 a number of overseas exchanges were negotiating to buy the voice-recognition system, which was developed by an Australian software house, Applied Financial Services, with the SFE, under licence from Verbex Voice Systems Inc.

The SFE believes future opportunities for expansion will be linked closely to the growth in over-the-counter risk-management products—financial products tailored to individual

Chief executive Les Hosking surrounded by the fallout of a long day's trading on the SFE floor.

customers' needs. With growth continuing in risk-management instruments such as options and swaps, the SFE is confident that futures trading will continue to derive benefit from the financial and business community's increased awareness of the need to manage risk. As banks increasingly provide hedging and risk-management products for their clients, they will also increasingly turn to futures markets for their own protection and reduction of counterparty risk. Futures markets, with their standardised contracts, are not suitable for over-the-counter markets—which raises the next big question: should futures exchanges devise more flexible option products? Such a development, if it occurs, will move slowly, according to Les Hosking: 'One thing we have learned over the past seven years is that diversification can thin out market liquidity. And it is the big, liquid markets that draw users to futures.'

10
Unsung heroes

While much of the credit for the Sydney Futures Exchange's growth and development belongs to a handful of key, high-profile players—Clive Hall, Desmond Brook, Dick Newman, David Rutledge, John Oliver, Les Hosking—a continuing contribution has also been made by a succession of unsung heroes who served on the board and the various committees and sub-committees, helped develop new contracts and in other ways contributed to the size and stature of the present SFE. Along the way, a diverse membership has been willing, in the interests of ensuring a viable futures market and raising the profile of the SFE, to work with changes and new rules.

Over the years, the SFE, being a non-profit organisation owned by its members, has drawn on a wide pool of expert volunteers to develop and design contracts. The exchange has relied on users of its markets, as well as members, to develop and design contracts that meet market demand. The growth of the SFE is reflected in the increase in the number and size of committees which in 1979, when bank bill futures were listed as the exchange's fourth contract, numbered eight. They were committees for wool, cattle, precious metals, financial instruments (which then comprised a mere four people), public relations and education, articles and by-laws, premises and the trading floor. A finance committee was introduced in 1980. Next established was the committee for inspection and audit (CIA), convened by John Oliver, then chairman of the SFE, chief executive David Rutledge and board member Frank Ryan. In 1983 a committee on registered representatives was added, bringing the total to eleven. During 1984 the number ballooned to eighteen with the addition of an executive committee and committees dealing with insurance, regulation, locals, exchange-traded options, the Comex link and membership. The following year an interstate committee was established. From 1986 the number of committees continued to rise. During the late 1980s the financial products committee at times included twelve or fourteen people as well as groups of six or eight on each of the several sub-committees. The financial products committee was outdone in size in 1989 by the clearing steering committee under Bruce Hudson, which that year numbered seventeen participants.

As new contracts were contemplated, or a fresh development or hurdle arose, a committee would be established to deal with the issue. Generally, each committee included an SFE board member, often as convenor, a number of floor and associate members, a representative of the relevant industry and an SFE staff member as secretary. The committees have performed an important function as a point of contact between members and the SFE, a conduit for the emerging views of the market to the board of the exchange. Committee reports are sent to the board, which examines a range of issues including new members, associate members, complaints, clearing, legislation, standards of behaviour, code of conduct and contract specifications. In this way the committees have helped shape exchange policy. The time absorbed by committee meetings has varied depending on the task; members would meet frequently when, say, designing a new contract or dealing with a specific problem. The role of the committees increased as the 1980s got under way, especially concerning the development of new financial products.

In the early days, when wool was the sole contract, the structure of operations at the exchange was generally far less formal than it was later to become. The start of work on the cattle contract signalled the beginning of a trend that was to see the SFE increasingly benefit from outside technical advice. The committee charged with devising the cattle contract included John Cooper of Sanger Australia Pty Ltd—who went on to serve for many years on the cattle committee—Norm Lethbridge of Dalgety Australia Ltd and Barry Noble of the large beef wholesalers G.M. Scott Pty Ltd, as well as John Hooton from the SFE. An additional adviser was John Weeks, then a stock-and-station agent at Homebush. The cattle committee, under its chairman David Marina (an SFE board member from 1979 to 1988), continually grappled with the task of trying to devise contract specifications that would please everyone; the contract was unusually vulnerable to vested interests, relying as it did on highly subjective judgments about what made cattle acceptable for delivery.

The gold committee, established in 1978, worked on devising the gold contract, its specifications and how it would trade. The SFE received assistance from Bert Aitken of Matthey Garrett Pty Ltd and Geoffrey Robinson of the Perth Mint. Andy McConnel, who convened the gold committee, recalled that he and Desmond Brook spent considerable time in discussions with Aitken and Robinson. 'There was no such thing then as a 50 oz gold bar,' said McConnel. 'The Perth Mint, Bert Aitken and Engelhard Industries moulded one specially for the SFE. And Bert was very helpful regarding security, to ensure that no "lead sandwich" got into the system.'

Those involved in the protracted attempt to get currency futures off the ground in the early 1970s reaffirmed their support in 1976. At that stage AML&F, Hill Samuel and MBC International (later BA Australia) offered to contribute financially to the SFE's investigations in a bid to hasten the launch of a concept that was welcomed in the financial community but for years blocked by government and Treasury.

Disappointment with progress on currency futures fuelled the determination of the SFE to launch a financial futures contract and work began on what was to become the 90-day bank-bill futures contract. The committee established to examine the question included Andy McConnel, Bob Wright, David Greig, Gerry van Wyngen and Les Pegg. Pegg, then head of money market operations at AGC, had previously worked at Bill Acceptance Corporation with Philip Miskin, founding father of the Australian commercial bill market, and he well understood the mechanics of the bill market. McConnel, who had been a driving force in establishing a gold contract, was also an energetic proponent of bank-bill futures. Never a details man, McConnel nonetheless carried out enormous groundwork to get the bill contract established. The SFE encountered considerable goodwill in the financial markets, receiving generous help from several leading figures in the short-term money market, some of whom had no involvement in futures at that time but whose companies would subsequently become members and major players in financial futures. Several senior money-market staff at the Commonwealth Bank, notably Kevin O'Donnell, David Williams and Ed Condran, helped with details of delivery and settlement and were instrumental in securing agreement from the bank's management to have the Commonwealth Bank act as settlement agent, confirming the integrity of the bills offered for delivery. The involvement of the Commonwealth Bank, given its dominant role in the bill market, gave an imprimatur to the new contract.

In the early 1980s a huge effort was put in by the articles and by-laws committee, whose members worked long hours with the SFE's legal advisers, Laurence & Laurence, to construct a revamped legal framework for the exchange. Next came the launch of the share-price index (SPI) futures contract, overseen by a committee convened by Bruce Hudson of Ord Minnett. The SPI contract brought the SFE to the attention of the stockbrokers and aroused some petty jealousies among the SFE members—a diverse group of whom many were unwilling to share the cake, unable to grasp the reality that, far from the stockbrokers stealing business, the SFE was gaining a new dimension that would build a bigger futures market.

Work had already begun on the possible launch of a bond contract. The minutes of a meeting of the financial instruments committee record that in 1980 Les Pegg and Warwick Poulden were to work on a paper discussing the possibilities of a two-year bond contract. A bond contract was not possible with the tap-and-tender system, where interest rates on the bonds were set by the Reserve Bank, but the move to a tender system, where rates would be set by the market, was in prospect.

In July 1985 the various financial committees—share-price index, financial instruments committee and exchange-traded options committee (formed in 1984)—were brought together

Phil Gray—longest-serving committee member and many times chairman of the financial products committee.

as the financial products committee, which was to play a pre-eminent role during the remainder of the decade. Phil Gray takes the bouquet as the longest-serving member of that committee, which at times he chaired. (Gray, who traded the first bill strip in 1980, was also instrumental in bringing three banks into the SFE membership: the Commonwealth, Australian Bank and State Bank NSW). Other chairmen of the financial products committee included Phil Gardiner, Chris Talbot, Kevin Jameson, Bruce Hudson, Ralph Carstairs and Ric Spooner. By 1986 the committee had spawned various sub-committees for bonds, currency, linkages, options and the share-price index. In 1990 and 1991 the financial products committee was broken down into separate committees each representing a contract, for example a 90-day bank-accepted bill committee chaired by Dave Pearson, a bond committee headed by Rob Stewart, a share-price index committee chaired by Steve Knapp, an options committee chaired by John Jarratt and a cattle committee headed by Colin Wright.

By the mid-to-late 1980s membership of an SFE committee carried enviable status. This contrasted with the earlier years, when the SFE was struggling to expand with limited internal resources and serving on a committee—as many selflessly did—was not a role widely sought. The SFE was fortunate in having a hard core of committed and willing workers, interested volunteers who were keen to see the markets develop. In the 1980s, particularly during the mid-1980s when there was considerable product development, elections to SFE committees became toughly fought campaigns as members sought to ensure that their interests were represented.

Key questions to be dealt with as the 1980s progressed were the landmark move to negotiable commissions and the introduction of local members, each of which was addressed by a committee which reported to the board.

A locals committee was established in 1984 to oversee the introduction of local members. This was initially convened by Desmond Brook and included Les Pegg, Bill King and David Marina, with King and Marina going on to become the SFE's first two local members. Members accommodated the introduction of locals whose growth is seen as inseparable from continuing success for the SFE. Several floor members have facilitated clearing for locals; for example, Tullett & Tokyo and McIntosh Futures Ltd clear for locals and L Quay Futures Brokers Pty Ltd was established in November 1991 as a specialist on the floor clearing for locals. Early in 1993 L Quay ranked tenth in terms of volumes traded on the exchange and locals accounted for some 14 per cent of SFE business.

A watershed for the SFE during the late 1980s was the question of self-clearing. Considerable controversy surrounded the change in clearing arrangements, with many members satisfied with the ICCH system and many others taking the view that the SFE would be better off carrying out its own clearing. In the end, members praised the SFE's handling of the change and the formation of the Sydney Futures Exchange Clearing House (SFECH). To help smooth the process, a large clearing steering committee was established under the chairmanship of Bruce Hudson. The objective was to get people involved, exchange views and secure feedback about what was seen as a radical move. In what amounted to a trial run, a clearing advisory committee was appointed to carry out some of the functions that would be expected of a clearing-house board. An extensive clearing services committee under Kevin Tinker examined systems for allocating, confirming and clearing trades.

The committees listed in the annual reports reflect the change of direction and emphasis for the SFE. Apart from committees dealing with issues related to specific contracts and areas such as the trading floor and education, there was significant growth in committees overseeing issues such as membership, regulation and clearing.

Over the years the committees have had to wrestle with some challenging issues and overcome testing episodes. As was the case with the cattle squeeze in 1982, they have had to deal with situations that had no precedent, where there was no easy rule book to follow. A thorny question that arose over the bank-bill futures contract concerned which banks were of a suitable status to have their paper accepted for delivery. Initially it was envisaged that the futures market would allow only bank bills issued by the major trading banks to be acceptable for delivery. This was based on the convention that the paper of these banks ranked *pari passu* in the market, and that the futures market should follow commercial market practice. The state banks, though, resented any suggestion that their paper was of inferior quality. At that stage there was no question of any state banks being in trouble; the decision to exclude their paper from delivery reflected the fact that the infant bill futures market needed to be based on a homogeneous product, and that by convention, state banks' paper traded at a higher yield than that of a major bank. Further, at a time when state banks did not have interstate branches, location could be a problem for bills payable outside Sydney. Also, in the early days of the bill contract the SFE was still struggling to build its credibility and the contract itself was yet to acquire the status it achieved in the 1980s. Corporates were still reluctant to trade. The SFE was unwilling to take any step that might detract from the strength of the bill contract. Its preference was to bring in new banks as the market developed.

The state premiers let the SFE know that they did not like having their banks' paper slighted by being excluded. State Bank of Victoria wrote requesting inclusion, as did Bank of Queensland. Rural Bank of NSW (now State Bank NSW) was the first state bank to have its paper accepted. A further chink was made in the wall when the newly formed Australian Bank Ltd applied to have its paper accepted and was admitted in December 1982. Early in the following year the financial instruments committee rejected applications from Bank of Queensland and Bank of New Zealand. The issue ebbed and flowed. Then, in 1985 the newly established Macquarie Bank (previously the merchant bank Hill Samuel Australia Ltd) applied to have its paper accepted for delivery. Its application was followed by one from Rural & Industries Bank of WA. With new banks on the horizon, the SFE realised that these applications would be the first of many. A sub-committee was established in October 1985, chaired by Chris Talbot, to consider appropriate criteria for approving applications to the list of approved acceptors for the bank-accepted bill futures contract. The committee noted that the SFE could adopt a similar method to that used on the IMM for the domestic certificate of deposit (CD) contract. This would require the financial instruments committee to approve a list of market participants which would be asked by the exchange to list ten players which, in their opinion, were the most active in the bank bill and CD market. These ten would be designated 'dealers' and from them the exchange was to select seven and ask them which banks' acceptances, trading at the same yield, carried the highest liquidity and lowest credit risk. Those banks whose names were common to five of the lists would be designated as approved acceptors. However, the issue of nominating ten 'best' players and then selecting a further group was highly political; every time the financial instruments committee thought it had found a solution, a new problem developed and more lobbying ensued. In the end, and despite considerable and often heated discussions that continued for years, the SFE took the view that there was no point in changing the delivery features of a contract that was trading as successfully as bank-bill futures. Apart from broadening delivery to include certificates of deposit from acceptable banks, the highly successful bank-accepted bill futures contract is largely unchanged from what was originally devised in 1979.

The bond committee has had to cope with a number of potentially damaging episodes, including allegations of market manipulation by major players. Initial debates concerned whether the proposed bond contract should be deliverable or not: if deliverable, what bonds to deliver and if not, what to use as a cash-settlement price. After much deliberation it was decided to launch a two-year bond because, it was said, that would meet market demand. And the authorised dealers were expected to make more use of a two-year, rather than a longer, bond. However, by the time the contract was launched the shape of the yield curve had changed and five and ten-year bonds had become more popular. Activity from the authorised dealers fell short of expectation. So a ten-year bond contract was introduced and was very successful, becoming one of the SFE's key contracts until, in 1988, the supply of ten-year bonds began to decline because of a reduction in government borrowings. A three-year bond contract was introduced as a solution. This could have met the same fate as its two-year predecessor; however, Westpac took the view that the contract, in offering a chance to hedge in a particular area of the yield curve, was vital for portfolio management. Terry Toohey, then head of Westpac's fixed-interest department, his senior dealer Peter Kelly and the rest of the dealing team are credited with creating enough volatility to boost the contract's liquidity and save it from potential extinction. The three-year bond contract went on to become one the SFE's success stories.

An area where members have helped create a new dimension in futures trading concerns EFPs (exchange-for-physical transactions). Most EFPs involve using the SFE's three-year and ten-year bond contracts to hedge trading in commonwealth and semi-government bonds. EFPs, which add to hedging flexibility, are estimated to account for between 10 and 15 per cent of the SFE's total volume. They are also credited with boosting liquidity in the swaps market, where they are particularly useful for those needing to hedge a large exposure.

SFE members have played a role in education and marketing. Some members have been critical of the SFE for not spending more on marketing. However, the SFE has always been sensitive to the views of members who did not wish to see the exchange spend their funds on promotion which the members could undertake themselves. The early efforts to market the wool contract to a reluctant farming community were replicated later with courses and seminars explaining how financial futures worked. These were successful in broadening the range of users in the financial community but struck some resistance in the corporate sector. Between the wool era and the dominance of financial futures were the cattle and gold years, which encouraged a different type of member from the earlier 'woollies'. The introduction of the cattle contract brought in more speculative traders and some colourful personalities to the SFE; the launch of the gold contract took the SFE into the retail market, giving it a high profile among the general public.

Darlington is credited with giving the SFE its biggest push into the retail market. Riding on the back of the gold boom, the company became the largest retail futures broker, backed by enormous research and huge resources in terms of technical analysis at a time when that was rare in Australia. Ross McConnel Kitchen also developed considerable retail business, as did Nichols and later Jacksons. RMK's Murray Carr carried out considerable marketing in gold and bank-bill futures, and went on to serve on the SFE's marketing committee, convened at that time by Ric Spooner. As the gold rush evaporated and the SFE increasingly identified with financial futures, the marketing thrust has been more towards the professional and institutional, rather than retail, market. However, a few brokers cater for the retail sector, such as Ord Westpac, which operates with a substantial base of sophisticated private clients.

Bankers Trust Australia, as the merchant bank BT Australia, was one of the first in the financial markets to join the SFE, becoming a floor member in 1979. Bankers Trust, whose initial push into futures was handled by Warwick Poulden, spent considerable energy in marketing the concept to its professional clients, compiling and distributing explanatory brochures and holding seminars outlining how interest-rate futures operated. Poulden served for several years on the SFE's financial instruments committee, as well as on the committees for public relations and education, and marketing. BT was an example of the merchant banks which joined the SFE and energetically drummed up business in a way that broadened the client base of the exchange. Innovators in their day, the wooltraders were not familiar with financial markets and, moreover, were generally very small operations unable to compete with the volatility and volumes seen in the 1980s. According to Poulden, BT's approach was three-pronged: to educate the professional market about futures and act as broker to them; to encourage the institutional market to hedge and to cover the retail market indirectly through stockbrokers. Other members have enthusiastically marketed SFE products and potential to institutions, particularly John Craig at Tullett & Tokyo and Chris Gorman at Ord Westpac, with Gorman undertaking considerable overseas marketing, notably to the managed funds.

By the late 1980s and early 1990s the SFE was comfortably operating with an increased in-house legal and technical staff, as well as with its own research and development team. But it has maintained its lines of communications to members and users through a network of committees whose existence continues to be of mutual benefit.

Postscript

The history of the Sydney Futures Exchange is one of meeting, and overcoming, challenges. More lie ahead, including the process of globalisation and rationalisation, the growth of over-the-counter products, the increase in the number of locals and choice of contracts.

The exchange entered the 1990s with a solid platform on which it built further in terms of developing its own clearing arrangements and extending after-hours trading. The heavy capital costs of computer development in the five years to 1992, totalling $13.5 million, produced upgraded systems for price-reporting, trade-matching, allocation and confirmation of trades, clearing and trading on SYCOM. The equivalent of this outlay was saved by SFECH in its first year of operation. 'That $13.5 million was well spent,' says Les Hosking. 'It improved the core business of the exchange's futures and options market. And our strategic plan got us where we wanted to be. Now we can identify new areas to plumb.'

To Hosking there are opportunities in the worldwide growth of over-the-counter products. In the same way that growth in stockmarket trading feeds the share-price index contract, growth in the OTC market is expected to produce additional volume for futures markets. Moreover, it could lead to a greater demand by OTC markets for exchange-related practices in clearing and trading, such as screen dealing.

Rationalisation and globalisation will come from the desire on the part of futures exchanges to see their members' exposures to different markets reduced. Logic dictates a rationalisation of exposures across different markets. That leads to the idea of a 'super-clearer' which would clear futures, options and other derivatives under one roof, with sophisticated margining, guaranteeing and clearing services. The considerable commonality among derivatives, within countries and across countries, will be the factor driving market development. The trend towards offsetting risks will be driven by exchanges or their members. Inevitably there will be a rationalisation of exchanges and clearing houses—it is happening already.

A facility to offset exposures in different markets would have alleviated much of the tension associated with the 1987 stockmarket crash. The cash market gridlocked and those with losing positions could not pay. A 'super-clearer' could have offset profits and losses in a way that would have enabled a greater volume of transactions to be processed.

Over the past twenty years exchanges have been seeking new contracts to increase turnover, whereas in fact their future growth might well depend on identifying different ways to lift profitability for members and improve their own balance sheets. The SFE's decision to take over its own clearing arrangements enabled its members to become clearers, securing a new source of income for themselves by providing a service to the market.

Futures exchanges' clearing houses provide facilities where traders can deal without having to worry about counterparty risk—a major concern in OTC markets. Looking ahead, futures exchanges could sell their clearing expertise to non-futures areas. For example, the SFE could sell its trading and clearing services and could create additional services to sell to other markets. Futures markets discover prices better than any other sector. The SFE could diversify by selling its information and expertise.

Market regulation and supervision remains a major concern. The regulators are conscious that the law lags financial markets developments such as the explosion in derivative products. The regulators will be supportive of any move that diminishes counterparty risk and enhances the capital position of players; thus they could be expected to approve of a trend towards mutual clearing arrangements and offsets.

Futures exchanges will continue in their encouragement of local traders. By early 1993 the SFE operated with 130 locals, a group of well-capitalised individual traders providing a vital pool of liquidity for the exchange's markets, who accounted for between 15 and 18 per cent of its business. Locals are by definition always ready to trade so the exchange operates with a mix of players who are there all the time because trading is their livelihood. Having a diversified group of players leads to different approaches, which makes a market.

The SFE plans to expand its fraternity of locals but realises that this is a long-term plan. It takes generations to develop a core of wealthy and profitable locals, but the SFE is well on track.

Index